BORN TO DO IT

Becoming the Leader of a Business Niche Using Powerful Spiritual Techniques

DR REBEKAH LOUISA SMITH

First printing: 2020

ISBN-13: 978-0-9956849-8-0

Published by Butterfly House Publishing:
www.butterflyhousepublishing.com

British Cataloguing Publication Data: A catalogue record of this book is available from The British Library.

Also available for Kindle from Amazon.

WHAT PEOPLE ARE SAYING ABOUT *BORN TO DO IT*

"This is the business book I've been looking for all my life."

Charlotte Atkinson
Film Producer and Career Coach

"Rebekah relays her understanding of what it takes to be successful, offers the components to help make it happen, and, most importantly, truly wants to help by guiding one to their success!"

Nand Harjani
CEO and Founder of Creative Life Sciences

"Rebekah's story is so motivational! She has written a really useful book, containing everything the reader needs to get to where they want to be and to help them run their business efficiently, not just as a growing business owner in the film industry but also on a spiritual and personal level with transferable information for many other small to medium enterprises. A must have and a must-read book!"

Gerlanda Milioto
Business Strategist

"An invaluable, informative guide with a spiritual twist, for the budding business entrepreneur."

Christine Chambers
Professional Intuitive Spiritual Mentor

"Rebekah doesn't just talk the talk when it comes to the soul's journey and business, and this book is proof. She has gifted the world with her courage and now she's sharing her experience to help other people."

Nicole Bonomi
Film Producer

"Born To Do It *is packed with essential tips, inspiring personal stories, and spiritual guidance to help entrepreneurs connect to their purpose, find their niche, and build a successful business based on human connection and kindness. From logo Feng Shui, to personalized pitches, to the power of positive thinking, to creating budgets and pipelines, Dr Smith generously, and with beautiful vulnerability, serves up the goods in this gem of a book."*

Jessica Graham
Author of *Good Sex: Getting Off Without Checking Out*

"I loved this book and read it in one sitting. I found it fascinating and couldn't believe that after 10 years of friendship with Rebekah there is so much I didn't know. It is interesting for both people who know her well and for those who have never met her. I loved the way she talks in it; it feels like a discussion.

Help books, particularly about business, I often find to be quite condescending and demanding. This is definitely not that. It feels like the sharing of ideas. I love the first-hand stories; it makes it feel so relatable and approachable. I like that even for me, who can be a little sceptical about spirituality, it is interesting and still relevant. I was particularly interested in the quantum color technique. It's a great idea and one you can see every day. I like how Rebekah acknowledges those who have helped her along the way. It's a great book and I really enjoyed reading it."

Talia Clarke
History of Art Expert

"Born To Do It *is a book of AFFIRMATIONS about what you are doing right, ILLUMINATIONS about the soul purpose yearning to manifest and IMPACTFUL AWAKENING about environments you should turn your back on!"*

Dr Maboreng Maharaswa
Entrepreneur and Content Producer

DEDICATION

I dedicate this book with love and gratitude to our best friend, the Universe, who always takes care of us.

I also dedicate this book to my family, everyone who is part of my tribe and of course to you, my inspirational leader.

CONTENTS

FOREWORD

My friend introduced me to Rebekah at a networking event. "This is Dr Rebekah Louisa Smith; she has a PhD in Tarantino," she said. I think we can agree this is hard to beat as a qualification if you are going to grow the most successful film festival strategy consultancy business in the world, whose purpose is to help filmmakers win festival awards. With over 800 such awards under her belt after 10 years of building her brand and her empire, we can safely say that Rebekah Louisa Smith is The Film Festival Doctor.

It takes much more than a vision to start a business, as we all know. Passion. Check. Enthusiasm. Check. Knowledge. Check. Rebekah is the very embodiment of a new breed of entrepreneur. Defining her brand on her own terms, she is succeeding in the most creative and complex of fields. Ask Rebekah "Why film?" and she'll tell you about her early experiences and the decisions she made.

Filmmakers may be great during the creative process but what about after they finish their film – what's next? Over the years, during the time I've been around filmmakers, it's become clear to me that many think it's only about getting the film made. In a creative sense this is true, of course. However, it is reasonable to suggest that the main purpose of making a film is for it to be seen.

In a complex industry, the first major point of lift-off for any filmmaker is to enter a film festival. What better way could there be to test your credentials and gauge reaction to your work? Clearly, there are hundreds of festivals around the world. The real expertise comes from knowing exactly the best 'fit' for your work and focusing upon being accepted. Rebekah excels in this particular field, and the hundreds of wins achieved for her clients is testament to that. Any filmmaker lucky enough to engage her is in a great position to achieve the critical step of gaining recognition for their work.

As an entrepreneur, Rebekah has built an excellent team to support her commercial aims. Behind all this success lies a secret, which will be explored when you read this awesome book. Rebekah manifests her success on a daily basis. She'll explain how – and you'll discover that there are some crucial steps you can take to help you succeed with your business.

On a personal note, you'll find that this book captivates and inspires. It's a story of triumph and determination. As a friend, Rebekah is loyal and trusted. As a businesswoman, she carries these values into her work. You can be certain of one thing with Rebekah: she will get the job done. As John Travolta's Vincent Vega says in *Pulp Fiction*, "This is a moral test of oneself. Whether or not you can maintain loyalty. Because being loyal is very important."

Phil McCauley, Entrepreneur

PREFACE

Unexpectedly, during the COVID-19 pandemic of 2020, I became inspired to write. I was approached by an Indian publishing company who were compiling a book called *Unique: Positive Stories to Inspire You* and wanted me to share my life story. This was a brilliant book project and I accepted their offer as it was an opportunity for me to help people in situations I had experienced. I could talk about what I love doing most and also be very honest about how I got through challenging and difficult periods. I actually enjoyed the writing process much more than I expected, especially as I hadn't done any writing since I completed my PhD in 2011.

When the *Unique* book went live and was available to buy internationally, I was approached by Butterfly House about writing my own story to inspire others. After having a long hard think, I knew that, deep down, writing a book was exactly what I wanted to do. I was thrilled that people had engaged with my story and resonated with it and I received feedback from business owners who now felt very motivated to keep going and didn't feel alone. One reader said that the honesty of my story helped her reduce fears of loneliness and isolation whilst running her first business.

That's when the penny dropped! I love everything about the world of business, and I love doing what I was born to do – so I said "Yes!" to Butterfly House and told them I would be writing a different type of book. I wasn't interested in writing a dry 'how to start your first business' book that was very formulaic and had been done to death a million times. Rather, I wanted to write a book that showed people how to launch their first business using essential business practices and also drawing upon spiritual techniques that would help them discover their soul purpose and teach them how to co-create with the Universe. I wanted to help them create and run the business of their dreams.

Thank you for buying this book. I'm super excited for the journey ahead of you!

INTRODUCTION
BUSINESS MEETS SPIRITUALITY

Thank you so much for purchasing this book! I'm super excited to share this life-changing journey with you. I will be helping you to discover what you were born to do and showing you how to launch your business. This book is designed for people who have a passion for business and an entrepreneurial spirit; people who are also very interested in spirituality and are open to incorporating spiritual practices into their business. This book combines these two practices and shows you how to create an abundant business and cultivate an abundant mindset using both standard business methods and spiritual techniques.

Just before you dive in and start reading, let's do a little five-minute quick-fire questionnaire...

1. Are you willing to do whatever it takes?
2. Will you show up every day and put the work in?
3. Are you obsessed with your business (or your business idea)?
4. Are you committed to discovering what your soul purpose is?
5. Are you able to adjust your business model where necessary?
6. Are you committed to your business for life?

7. Are you willing to learn more about yourself through your business?
8. Are you willing to integrate spiritual techniques into your business?
9. Are you committed to being the face and leader of your brand?
10. Are you a quitter?

If you answered yes to questions 1-9 and no to question 10, carry on reading. If you answered yes to question 10, stop reading. And if you answered no to questions 1-9 then definitely stop reading.

So, let's begin.

Welcome to Born To Do It

My name is Dr Rebekah Louisa Smith (and yes, I'm a real doctor – PhD) and, as the CEO and founder of The Film Festival Doctor, I am one of the leaders in my niche. In a nutshell, we create successful film festival strategies for our clients, so they can get their film seen at film festivals around the world and win awards. My company has worked with hundreds of filmmakers. So far, we have helped our clients win over 800 awards on the festival circuit. I live in the USA and have a wonderful team of people who support me, both in my home town of Los Angeles and in the UK.

Being the leader of your business niche does not mean you need to put a ridiculous amount of pressure on yourself to be the best in your field and compete against your competitors; rather, it means you stand out from the crowd of people within your niche (including other entrepreneurs, business owners and your competitors etc.), no matter how big or small that crowd might be.

What does the term 'niche' mean with regards to starting up a business? A business niche is a specialized or focused area of a broader market that businesses can serve in order to differentiate themselves from their competitors. It is crucial for business owners to find a niche within their industry that has under-served or unmet needs – in other words, there is a gap in the market. This is what I'll be helping you to accomplish throughout this book.

One of the things you will rarely find within the literature of business start-up books is how to achieve success by integrating spiritual techniques into your business. In my eyes, and from my own experience, spiritual practices can make businesses thrive and I believe spirituality to be an integral part of a business' infrastructure. Throughout this book you'll learn techniques to help you become the leader of your business niche using spiritual practices associated with the law of attraction, including cosmic ordering, manifestation and Feng Shui.

Not so long ago, I'd never in a million years think I would write this book and be in a position to help nurture you on your journey into the worlds of business and spirituality. My original life plan was to complete my PhD, start a full-time career within academia teaching Film Studies, settle down and live in Wales. I was one of those girls who had her life all mapped out but then in 2009, by accident, I caught the 'film festival bug' and unexpectedly found my soul purpose and discovered what I was born to do.

At the time I wasn't aware of what a soul purpose was or what it meant – or even that this was, in fact, what I had discovered about myself – until I was introduced to the world of spirituality and the law of attraction three years later.

Your soul purpose is the reason you are here on earth. It gives you the drive and discipline to do the job you were born to do. Once you have identified what your soul purpose is, you'll then be able to live your dream and run the business that your heart and soul desires. I'll be referring to the soul purpose concept a lot throughout this book, as it is your soul purpose that acts as the backbone to help you become the leader of your business niche. It is also the driving force behind everything you do. I'll also be providing you with the tools you need to identify what your soul purpose is.

...

I caught the film festival bug while I was co-producing the 2009 Abertoir Horror Festival in Aberystwyth, Wales, where I was living and studying for my PhD. During the festival, I began to realize that my career ambitions were not in the world of academia but within the film industry, and my specialist area was film festivals. The skills I learnt and developed whilst writing my PhD (and also when I discovered my soul purpose) helped me identify a huge gap in the market that needed to be filled. A common problem for filmmakers was that they needed help getting their film seen at festivals; they didn't know how to do it, how to create a festival strategy or who to turn to for help resolving the problem.

At that time there was only one company that was actively providing this service and had a presence on the internet, the USA-based Film Festival Secrets. But I knew, deep down, that I could also help my target market resolve this pain. While working behind the scenes co-producing a film festival as well as travelling around Europe meeting lots of other festival programmers and learning how they curated their own festivals, I had discovered which type of films film festival programmers wanted to screen. Over canapes and champagne, I had learnt what a festival strategy looked like. There was a global market of filmmakers who needed help and support and I wanted to turn my knowledge into a business.

As I began to get my idea off the ground, I was consciously aware that I had no previous experience of running a business. However, through sheer determination, hard work and resilience, I didn't give up even when times were hard. My soul purpose kept me focused and was the thing that told me to never give in; it constantly and intuitively reminded me that this was what I was born to do. I was committed to both my business and my clients, who trusted me to work with them, and I knew that would never change.

My field of business is still very niche but that is not a problem, and my competitors and I continue to thrive. There is only a handful of companies around the world doing what my company does on a full-time basis.

The Film Festival Doctor quickly became a part of my identity and who I am. By 2012, I was known within my niche as 'The Film Doctor' or 'Rebekah Film Dr', both to my peers and colleagues and in the world of Instagram and social media.

How to Use This Book

I would advise you to read this book from start to finish, as I mention people and certain principles related to the worlds of business and spirituality as our journey progresses, and it will feel a bit fragmented and difficult to follow if you dip in and out or start halfway through the book and read backwards!

I have set you exciting tasks to complete at the end of each chapter, so we can get started on our adventure together whilst you're reading the book. By the end of it you'll have made a significant amount of progress developing your business model. You'll also have deepened your connection to the divine and will have a much clearer idea of your soul purpose and how to use spiritual methods.

Below is a breakdown of the structure of the book and what's explored within each chapter:

Chapter 1 - How to Discover Your Soul Purpose and What You Were Born to Do. The first thing you need to do before you set up your business is identify what it is that you are born to do – in other words, your soul purpose. This chapter explains the soul purpose concept and offers guidance and advice on how to successfully tap into it.

Chapter 2 - How to Find Your Niche. Now that you have identified your true calling and what it is that you are born to do, the next question you need to unpack is: can I make a living and create a business from it? This chapter draws upon techniques created by business consultant Ed J C Smith to help you identify your niche and whether it can work as a business.

Chapter 3 - How an Epic Fail Can Become One of Your Most Successful Services. This chapter stresses the importance of sticking to your niche and not deviating from your soul purpose. Here I discuss how I created a separate business to resolve a different problem my clients had. However, as much as I really wanted to be the person to resolve it, this job was not what I was supposed to be doing. The experience helped me understand better what my clients wanted, which led to a much more successful solution to their problem.

Chapter 4 - Why Energetic Branding is Important for You and Your Business. This is the first chapter that discusses how to integrate spiritual techniques into your business. We will be exploring globally renowned transformational teacher Marie Diamond's Feng Shui and the law of attraction with regards to your business branding; specifically, your company logo and your website.

Chapter 5 - How to Organize Your Business and Position Yourself as an Expert. Before you can start doing what you were born to do for your clients, it is very important to have a strong infrastructure for your own business, so it can operate as a business should. This is the first of two chapters introducing business systems and techniques suggested by business strategist Gerlanda Milioto.

Chapter 6 - How to Create an Effective Sales Pitch. Before you begin any work with a client, you need to close the business deal with them. This is achieved by crafting a very effective sales pitch. Drawing further on Gerlanda Milioto's techniques, this chapter discusses in detail what a sales pitch is and how to create one that will result in working with an abundance of clients.

Chapter 7 - How to Integrate Cosmic Ordering into Your Business. This is the second chapter to feature spirituality. It focuses on how to blend spiritual coach and author Ellen Watts' cosmic ordering method into your daily business practices, so you can get more of what you dream of for yourself, your clients and your business.

Chapter 8 - How to Integrate Manifesting into Your Business. Following on from the previous chapter, here we look at how to incorporate the powerful process of manifestation and vision boards into your daily business practices.

Chapter 9 - Tying It All Together! How to Love Doing What You Were Born to Do. In this chapter you'll read stories demonstrating how to tie together all the business and spiritual practices covered in the book. You'll also explore the feelings you'll tend to experience when your soul purpose starts to shine its light.

Conclusion - Now Go and Shine Your Light Around the World! A gentle reminder that you are now ready and super focused to do this!

...

Your journey doesn't stop when you've finished reading the book, either! Follow me on Instagram @borntodoitbook and share your stories with me. Tag me and I promise I will proudly share them with my tribe of followers so everyone can see your progress and growth.

I can also work with you on a one to one basis to help you tune into your soul purpose so you can do what you were born to do. You can visit my website for further information: www.rebekahlouisasmith.com or drop me an email at rebekah@rebekahlouisasmith.com.

And of course, for those of you who need help getting your film accepted into film festivals, The Film Festival Doctor can certainly help you with that. Feel free to get in touch via www.thefilmfestivaldoctor.com.

Right, so let's get going. Before you begin reading the first chapter, have your favorite notebook and pen beside you, so you can get stuck into the tasks and allow your creativity, desires and imagination to run wild.

1
HOW TO DISCOVER YOUR SOUL PURPOSE AND WHAT YOU WERE BORN TO DO

As I mentioned in the introduction, my original life plan (writing my PhD, becoming a doctor, working within the world of academia and living in Wales forever) went out of the window when I began working for the Abertoir Horror Festival in Wales, UK. It was only while writing this book I realized how dramatically my life has changed from that original plan: I now live in Los Angeles and over the past 10 years I have built an established niche brand within the independent film industry. It was an amazing revelation and, if you put time aside to complete the tasks at the end of each chapter, you'll be well on your way to experiencing such revelations too. By the time you finish this book, you'll have made significant progress towards launching your first business. I can't wait to hear how your journey progresses.

Here's the golden rule. In order to become the leader of your business niche and a successful entrepreneur, the first thing you have to do – before you do absolutely anything else – is discover what your soul purpose is; it's also known as your 'why'.

This chapter explains in further detail what a soul purpose is and how to tap into yours.

What is a Soul Purpose?

Psychic medium Amanda Linette Meder explains that your soul purpose is the reason you are here on earth. It is your soul purpose that gives you that drive and discipline to do the job you were born to do. Amanda explains that the soul purpose is what keeps most people aligned to their truth and motivated to wake up in the mornings; it also often gives business owners and entrepreneurs their customer base. She explains that if your customers see in you what your purpose is, they'll keep coming back to work with you.

When you are living your soul purpose your job never feels like work. This is because you love what you do, and you don't need to make any effort whatsoever to complete a day's work. When people see you doing what you love and what you were born to do, others will want to follow you and work with you, both as clients and as members of your staff.

It is very important to remember that EVERYONE has a soul purpose within them – it's not something only a handful of people have. Everyone was born to do something. Your soul purpose is inside you, waiting to be discovered. It is a deep inner calling unique to each and every individual on the planet.

In their book *The Soul Purpose Method,* Licia Rester and Kirk Souder explain that the three key things a soul purpose presents to us when one has tapped into it are: (1) feeling vibrantly alive (that thing that gets us out of bed each morning, as Amanda described above); (2) learning and growing (we commit to giving our all); and (3) being of service by making a meaningful contribution to the world. In our case, as we are using the term 'soul purpose' in a business context, it means making a meaningful contribution to your niche; finding a gap within your industry that needs your attention and filling it with your knowledge, gifts and expertise.

Identifying your soul purpose is one of the hardest things to do, as it's not always obvious at first; it's also not often anything you consciously look for either. Amanda Linette Meder suggests a way to do this is to ask yourself the following questions:

- Is there an activity that makes you lose all sense of time? A craft that you work on where, when you step into it, hours pass?
- What do you wake up drawn to?

She recommends taking a few days, a week or a month to observe what brings you joy and what makes you feel excited. When you have found and begin living your gift, time becomes irrelevant and you find yourself working straight through lunch and well past dinner time. She explains that your soul's mission on earth is to find out how to discover your purpose, live your dream and imbue your life with the most joy, love and happiness. Essentially, every business owner who wakes up every working day excited is living their soul purpose.

A colleague of mine, a film producer named Charlotte, explained how she discovered her soul purpose.

"I owe my entire filmmaking career to my mum - not just for being supportive and helpful and believing in me and my crazy ideas, but for actually suggesting working in film.

My entire plan (seriously, since the age of four) had been to work in theatre. Both my parents work in theatre, so it was my whole world. I went from wanting to be a dancer to lighting designer to stage manager. I trained in stage management and did work experience at some incredible places, but sadly my last work experience job ruined it for me because of the people I was working with.

Two years after finishing my A Levels I was living in Germany and moping around, my mum said, "Well, you like watching TV. Why don't you work in TV?"

That then became film after I got onto the BFI Academy at Rural Media and realized how much I loved producing. It was like I'd found my 'thing' and knew exactly what I was meant to do.

So, I signed up to a couple of job sites and marketed myself as a producer. Within six months, I'd produced three short films and was off. My goal was to get 10 credits by the end of the year; I'd done it by September.

I think you know when you've found what you're meant to do, and it's almost impossible not to put everything you have into it.

Since then I've produced shorts, a radio program, developed features, walked away from projects and still not worked in TV – all thanks to my mum."

Although Charlotte doesn't mention 'soul purpose' in her story (when she wrote it she was not aware of the concept until I explained it to her), what she describes is the process of how one discovers it. And by talking about how it was her mother who helped lead her towards living her dream and doing her 'thing', her story also demonstrates that other people can help you identify what your soul purpose is. Charlotte's story also shows that when you've found your 'why' (or, as she describes it, her 'thing'), that is what drives you to give your all to everything you do; in her case, film producing.

I took a huge life-changing risk to start my business, The Film Festival Doctor, instead of following a career in academia and it was my soul purpose that was the invisible driving force behind my decision. My soul purpose gave me the confidence not to give up or listen to people telling me The Film Festival Doctor wouldn't work. It gave me the strength to believe in myself 100% and to move forwards and get it off the ground. When your soul purpose intuitively tells you this is what you need to do, nothing will stop you or hold you back.

When I began working for the Abertoir Horror Festival I soon realized I had a passion for the film industry. However, never did I think my soul purpose would be within the film festival niche...

The Awesome Abertoir Horror Festival

The Film Festival Doctor would not exist if the director of the Abertoir Horror Festival, Gaz Bailey, had not created this wonderful event – and that's a fact. In a way, he's partly responsible for both helping me discover my soul purpose and creating my business. Sometimes I think: "What if Gaz had never created the Abertoir Horror Festival?" I would probably still be working within the world of academia and not living my dream or doing something I am really passionate about.

The Abertoir Horror Festival is one of the most unique 'one of a kind' film festivals in the world. It not only screens cutting edge and outstanding horror films, it also incorporates theatre, live presentations, book readings and live music. We always stayed out until 6 am at the infamous Inn on the Pier, a pub on the seafront where lots of amazing networking took place over beer and pizza. Gaz Bailey is brilliant at running the festival and I'm so proud of him and what he's achieved. My happiest memory of

Abertoir is when we screened a blaxploitation film called *The Human Tornado*. Gaz and I introduced the film dressed as 70s pimps! It was unforgettable. Gaz talked like a Southern Texas native and I stood next to him as his glamorous girlfriend – it was just like a scene from the film! Gaz, Rhys and Nia run the festival now; naturally, I stepped down as The Film Festival Doctor became a full-time job. It will always be my favorite film festival and I recommend it to everyone.

All of this was obviously a lot of fun and I have so many more amazing memories of that festival that I could share with you in a separate book. However, during all this fun and madness, I began to take film festivals and filmmakers more seriously and it was at this point that The Film Festival Doctor was conceived. As I mentioned in the introduction, the project management skills I developed whilst writing my PhD helped me identify that there was a huge gap within the film festival world that needed to be filled. I heard regularly that filmmakers needed help getting their film seen at festivals because they didn't know how to create a festival strategy for their film, or which festivals they should submit their film to, and they didn't know who to talk to about this annoying problem. The more I was drawn towards learning how festivals worked behind the scenes, the more I realized the person to talk to was me. I also realized I was in my element at film festivals; I felt more alive and inspired, and the hours always flew by. I was literally doing what I was put on this earth to do.

Suddenly, this made me question whether academia was my passion. Was this what I really wanted to do? I realized that, deep down, it wasn't. I noticed that when I had previously attended academic conferences I wasn't as engaged as other academics were; I didn't feel like I was part of their world or on the same wave length as everyone else. One of my friends said: "I just love the world of academia. There is no other industry like it, is there?" and that was when my gut instinct told me that this just wasn't for me. I didn't love the world of academia, I wasn't emotionally connected to it, it didn't excite me, and it wasn't something I could do for hours or work through lunch and dinner for. Therefore, it really wasn't what I was supposed to be doing. Academia is certainly very interesting; it holds an incredible amount of value and I'm proud of my PhD thesis. However, I didn't have a deep-rooted interest in it, and I didn't share my colleague's passion.

I began to question why I wanted to go into academia in the first place. Did I feel like I had to, because further education was what everyone else was doing after graduating from college? Yes, I had a vested interest in Quentin Tarantino and I'm proud of my PhD, but my heart wasn't in it to continue studying or working further in academia. It just wasn't what I was born to do or what I even wanted to do anymore. I loved project management work and I'm so grateful to the PhD process for strengthening my skills in this area. If I hadn't gone down the path of writing my PhD, then I would never have known how to identify gaps in the market and create award-winning strategies for our clients.

The day after the Abertoir festival finished, I knew the world of academia was no longer nurturing or feeding my soul's purpose and I had to let it go so I could listen to the messages the divine was trying to get through to me. I made a commitment to see my PhD through to the end but also to get The Film Festival Doctor business off the ground. And I started to research my competitors to see if there was anyone else with the same gifts as me.

Film Festival Secrets

It's very important to remember that no one else in the world shares your soul purpose. For example, two people who work in a hairdressing salon might do the same job and share a similar gift, but each hairdresser will always deliver a different type of hairstyle. Let's say you want your hair blow-dried. Both Hairdresser A and Hairdresser B blow-dry your hair brilliantly but the way they do it is not identical; your hair might look stunning whoever blow-dries it, but it looks stunning in two different ways. They both offer different types of value thanks to the way in which they have connected with, and been guided by, their own unique and individual soul purpose.

As I mentioned in the introduction, there was only one key competitor at the time when I was planning on launching my business, a company called Film Festival Secrets who had a presence online and a website offering their services to filmmakers. Back in 2010 LinkedIn, Facebook, Pinterest, Instagram and Twitter were not so widely used and nowhere near as popular as they are now, so the good old-fashioned website was what I used to explore how this company's business model worked. I unpacked it and stripped it down to analyze all the components, how it operated and if there was anything missing. Obviously, there are more companies now who offer similar services to The Film Festival Doctor and everyone is a lot more visible thanks to Facebook groups, the visual medium of Instagram and the business world of LinkedIn, etc.

Chris Holland is the man behind Film Festival Secrets. He is a pioneer in this niche and excellent at what he does. His book (also called *Film Festival Secrets*) is a brilliant resource for first time filmmakers who are keen to learn more about the festival circuit and the secrets behind how to get their film seen at festivals. Chris has a loyal following and is very well respected. I admire what he does and love his book, as it really is a good starting point; it's a very helpful and clear 'how to' guide.

Chris offered a range of consultancy services, including festival strategy creation and coaching calls, answering questions from filmmakers about the festival circuit. However, he didn't do film festival management – which was what I was planning on doing.

The film festival management service is very different to the film festival strategy consultancy service. The former involves a lot more work as, in addition to creating the festival strategy, we complete all the film festival submissions for the client, lobby their film directly to our contacts, organize all the festival screenings and provide professional support to the client during their festival journey.

By offering another service and another option to filmmakers, where I would be very hands on and more involved from start to finish, I could really help them achieve their goals. In addition, I could also help them at a level that was more committed compared to working as a consultant.

A friend of mine correctly pointed out that although this was good in theory, I had no successful business model to compare it to, or any success stories to talk about. Clearly, Christopher's success proved the consultancy service model works. I didn't have any evidence that a management service model would work too. At first, I thought, "Let's try it and see," but deep down I knew that wasn't the best idea as my business needed a business model to work from. Instead, I did my research and discussed my ideas with my target market while I was attending the world's largest film festival, the Cannes Film Festival, in May 2010.

The Cannes Film Festival Adventure

The glamorous Cannes Film Festival has been running since the 1930s and is the type of festival that everyone in the film industry attends. All the big Hollywood stars have walked the red carpet at Cannes and all the key players and movers and shakers go there to talk business over champagne in gorgeous five-star hotels.

The very first time I attended the Cannes Film Festival was in 2010 and I received lots of useful feedback from filmmakers about my business idea. The response was positive: everyone loved the idea -but many people were concerned that filmmakers wouldn't pay for the service until I proved it would work. They said I would need to work for free before I could start charging any money but that this would also help me to set the price for the service. I took this on board and that feedback really helped me to figure out the finer details of the management service. I did work for free on some projects, which was well worth the investment as it helped to prove that the service had the potential to work. After lots of fine tuning along the way, it is now one of my best-selling services.

The networking at Cannes is excellent; it's such a diverse festival and there is always someone interesting to meet. I met John, a producer, at a party and he became a very important part of my life and my business. John has been involved in my company since its inception; he was the person who supported me right from the beginning. We quickly developed a close bond and I could trust him. He always gave me advice when I needed it. He believed in me and what I was doing and was always available to support me. I can't thank him enough for his kindness and the way in which he helped me to become a stronger and more confident businesswoman.

When you have tuned into your soul purpose and you begin to live your dream, you become extremely resilient and disciplined about everything you do in your business and for your clients. As Charlotte suggested in her story, you will see things through to the end without ever giving up.

Despite the huge amount of effort I would need to put into The Film Festival Doctor to make it work, my soul purpose told me it would flourish and eventually I would find the tools to build it. And I was still giving my PhD 110%, despite my change of career.

My PhD supervisor, Martin, was not impressed with my decision, however. There was some tension between us as he was concerned I was too focused on the film industry and not giving my all to my thesis. Unfortunately, Martin couldn't see that The Film Festival Doctor was what I was meant to be doing. Eventually, we agreed to disagree, and he was pleased when I completed my studies and became a Doctor of Philosophy.

London Calling

In April 2011, I submitted my PhD thesis to the lovely Kath in the academic office, jumped into my car and drove to London to start my new life in England. I was going to build my business and live the life I had begun to create for myself, all the while being guided by my soul purpose. I had a basement flat in South East London ready to move into, the rent was a very good price, my awesome landlady was a film producer I met via the Abertoir Film Festival, and I could jump on the tube anywhere to access the entire city.

London is, of course, the capital city of the United Kingdom and the hub of the UK film industry. It's home to the infamous 3 Mills Studios, where many independent films were shot, including Guy Ritchie's *Lock Stock and Two Smoking Barrels* and *RockRolla,* and *Made in Dagenham*. Elstree Studios is where one of the UK's favorite soap operas *EastEnders* is filmed, and of course the oldest film studio Ealing Studios, which has made thousands of classic films since the 1930s, is also in London.

Lots of awesome film festivals are held in the UK, including the BFI London Film Festival, The London Short Film Festival, The Edinburgh International Film Festival, Underwire Film Festival, Open City Docs Fest and many more that I could get excited about. I wasn't able to grow my business in Wales, as the film industry there is tiny. In order to get my company on the map I needed to be in London, where all the action and networking events were taking place – so that was exactly what I did.

When I first attended networking events in London and talked about my business niche, I quickly realized that describing what I did and how I could resolve film festival strategy related problems was a skill in itself that one needs to learn in advance – and I learnt the hard way!

The next chapter will help you to avoid this, because it focuses on how to find your niche, how to figure out if your niche can work as a business and how to competently articulate your niche to others, so you can make it crystal clear that what you are born to do is important, because you are absolutely essential to help your client resolve their problem(s).

Exercises to Help You Become the Leader of Your Niche...

1. What is your soul purpose? Think long and hard about this but don't rush to answer the question as it may take some time and you might not be able to answer it right away. Refer back to Amanda Linette Meder's technique and make a few notes about what it is that makes you feel very excited and that you get lost in doing. Then let the answer come naturally to you without forcing it. Here are a few more follow up questions to help you...

2. What is your passion? What type of job could you do that doesn't feel like work?

3. What type of job could you do for hours and never get bored of?

4. If you are struggling, review Charlotte's story and ask yourself who could help inspire you to find your soul purpose.

NOTES

2
HOW TO FIND YOUR NICHE

Now you know how to discover your soul purpose, the next step is to figure out how to turn what you love to do (and what you were born to do) into a business.

As you now know, my niche is creating successful film festival strategies for filmmakers. Clearly that is *very* niche and is nowhere near as common as, for example, getting one's nails manicured at a beauty salon! However, a manicure is essentially a solution to a problem, which is exactly what a business does. Your soul purpose will help you fix your clients' problems in a way that no one else can.

For example, let's say you are an outstanding beauty therapist who is born to do this type of work. If a woman who is about to go to a party breaks a nail and is anxious to get it repaired before the party begins, then she has a problem that needs resolving. When she runs frantically into your salon and asks if you can fix her nail, it will still require you to explain to her how and why you are the best person (above all the other nail therapists in the area) to help her. Whatever area of business you work in you will need to clearly explain what you do and how you will resolve your client's pain in order to attract clients towards you and to then successfully close deals.

In this chapter I'll be drawing upon several essential techniques created by entrepreneur business coach Ed J C Smith. Before you can become the leader of your business niche and live your dream each day, you need to identify your niche, figure out if your niche will work as a business and then formulate your Big Domino Statement, so you can articulate your business and what you do to others. Ed's tools will help you do this with ease and during this process you'll learn a lot about how skilled and knowledgeable you are within your niche.

What Does A Film Festival Doctor Do?

When I first moved to London in 2011, I was asked this question all the time when I attended networking events and film festivals. I had such difficulty explaining to people what my business was and how we resolve our clients' problems.

The worst example was when a filmmaker asked me, "What does the Film Festival Doctor do?"

I replied: "It's kind of like a personal assistant service. We do everything for you and get your films into film festivals." Now that was garbled! When someone else asked the same question, I said "We get your film into film festivals and do everything for you!" And: "We help you get your film seen in festivals by sending it to the right people." Again, not really clear at all.

Eventually I got better. "We offer services to filmmakers to help them create successful film festival strategies." That got people interested and wanting to find out more. I'd then ask them something like: "Do you want to get your film seen at film festivals but don't know how to do it or have the right contacts? If so, we can help you resolve this problem by creating the right strategy for your film." This wasn't perfect, but it was an improvement and helped me to close my first few deals.

Between 2011-2012 my website was convoluted and not very clear, as everything was still in my head rather than on paper. At first it was far too wordy and it went around in circles, meaning visitors got bored and gave up. I could do what I wanted to do for my clients really well; it was setting out how I could help them that was the problem.

Eventually I met Ed J C Smith, who became one of my business coaches. Ed pointed out that what I was saying about my business and how I was positioning it needed to be clearer and much more punchy; he felt I was not positioning myself as an expert in my field.

Ed J C Smith and his Essential Finding Your Niche Techniques

Ed is the co-founder and director of a company based in the UK called the Champion Academy. Ed and his team teach business owners and entrepreneurs how to be more successful in their careers and develop their businesses. Ed's training courses are incredible, as he helps you learn how to maximize the value in everything you do for your clients, and how to think more clearly and take action in order to develop deeper communication skills. Ed is also the king of Facebook marketing – he even knows the people who run Facebook personally, so he's obviously well connected! I highly recommend his Facebook marketing courses if you want to go down this route. He's definitely the right person to show you how to get results and market your product effectively. His courses, which focus upon the psychology behind Facebook marketing, give you all the secrets behind this form of advertising and how to create your adverts in a way that will help you get more clients.

Ed is also one of the most generous and passionate people I've ever met. He commits to every client he works with 110% in order to help them reach their goals and every time you speak with him, he always reminds you to "never give up on your dreams". Ed recently published a book called *Money Mindfulness,* which he currently gives away for free on his website (you can find the link on the Resources page). It's a very useful and engaging read that will help you develop the right approach and attitude towards appreciating and accepting money and how to bring it into your life and your business.

I first met Ed at an event he was hosting where he was talking about how he could transform businesses that were not making money into generating a six-figure turnover. After meeting him in person, I knew I could trust him to work with me as he was kind and very driven to help me get results. When he was speaking, I knew he was the kind of person who would go the extra mile and ensure that you were supported, and his advice would be useful, no matter what. In no way was he one of those coaches who was not who he said he was: he had the results and authenticity behind him to prove he was genuine.

Ed has been part of my business since 2016 and he has seen it grow rapidly. I still work with him now from time to time and he's the one to thank for the awesome online group coaching program I offer. He gave me the tools to create this type of product through his *Clients on Automation* online course. This course is a comprehensive program that shows you how to create and market an online group coaching product that can turn over a minimum of US $10K a month or more.

At the beginning of the program, Ed stresses that it is very important to ask yourself several questions before you start to plan and subsequently launch your business. The first set of questions revolve around choosing your niche.

Why You Need to Pick Your Niche

Ed's training is very straightforward and clear. He breaks down the concept of a business into simplistic forms and removes all the complexities around starting one. Ed was the person who showed me that running a business is essentially all about solving a problem for your client. When you remember this every day, it really helps you to position and align your business to your ideal clients.

At the start of the course Ed explains that the first thing you must do before anything else is pick your niche. He asks you to think hard about the following questions:

What niche are you an expert in? There are thousands of niches – for example, blogging, buying and selling houses, wealth management, fashion, beauty and, in my case, film. Your soul purpose will always guide you towards the niche you have the most knowledge and experience in and are passionate about. And if you are still struggling to discover what your soul purpose is, this technique of Ed's can really help you to pinpoint what it is specifically.

In which niche are you most equipped to help people? Let's say, for example, you are very knowledgeable and have experience working within the world of social media. It's an area you know a lot about; it is what you were born to do. However, which area do you know the most about within that niche? Is it how to use Facebook to grow your business? Or Instagram? Or Twitter? Maybe it's how to create video content for effective social media promotion, or coaching people how to use LinkedIn, etc. Think about which micro area of your niche you are most passionate about. In my case, obviously it is film festivals.

Which niche are you most passionate about teaching? This is where your soul purpose takes center stage, and you can narrow the list you made for the previous question to just one key area. Let's say you are drawn towards Facebook because this is the area of social media where you can add the most value as you know more about it than the other platforms. It's also the area you are most passionate about compared to LinkedIn and Instagram, etc.

In which laser-focused aspects of this niche are you an expert? Do you feel you have the knowledge, experience and capability to teach people how to create and make money for their business via Facebook advertising, or how to create content for effective Facebook marketing, or how to use Facebook to build a loyal following, or how to create and manage a Facebook business page, or how to network effectively for your business using Facebook, etc.? Really narrow this part down to be very specific, streamlined and focused.

What are you most equipped to help people with? After breaking down the above questions into smaller pieces, perhaps you realize that what you were born to do is to help teach people how to create and make money for their business via Facebook advertising. In addition, you are already a leader in this niche because you have the knowledge and experience and you will be able to get your clients the results they desire.

Ed says that the area of your niche you are most equipped to help people with is the area where you will thrive and grow and become the leader of your niche – in this example, you will become the go-to person who can grow people's businesses and make substantial profits via Facebook advertising. However, before you go any further there is one more part of the process that must be completed...

Does Your Niche Work?

The next step is to think long and hard about whether your niche will be able to work as a business. This is something everyone should think about – if there is no market or demand within your niche, it won't be a viable business.

Ed asks you to consider:

Do people already make money from this niche? Referring back to the Facebook marketing example, the answer is a big yes – as lots of people already do it.

Is the niche growing or declining? Clearly the Facebook marketing model is growing rapidly as social media is a powerful tool for businesses to grow their client base.

Is there a demand for something different in this niche? Yes – in our example this would be the perfect opportunity for you to step in and show how small businesses can make a profit through Facebook marketing. And if you can offer a different service, it means people will pay for it.

Why is the old way less effective? After doing your research, your soul purpose will help you to identify that not every method people suggest for Facebook marketing is effective for everyone's business and the areas they work in. Let's say you have identified that small business owners who applied the standard Facebook marketing techniques to market their business services didn't make any money from it at all; they got no new business leads or sales and didn't get a return on their investment after spending a lot of money. You know how to solve this problem as you have the gifts that can help them achieve success and results for their business – this is where you and your services come in to fill that gap in the market and resolve this type of pain for your client.

Why is your new method more effective? To prove your method is more effective, you need to create a business that solves a specific problem and then articulate your niche to others. It's important to test your model and get some good results before you launch your business in order to prove it's a viable model. Once you have results, you can prove to potential clients that your method works and will heal their pain. This also means they will be happy to pay you, as you are a valuable asset to them.

The technique above should always be completed before you launch a new business. It's extremely important to know if there is a market and demand for your niche and whether there are people who have the funds to pay for your services. If demand is low, you won't have a sustainable business.

I will never forget what Ed taught me, which I repeat to myself every day and when I'm closing deals with prospective clients. Every single business revolves around solving problems and healing their clients' pain. You provide a product or service that helps them to fix their problem. Ed encouraged me to create what he calls a 'killer problem statement', which becomes the core element around which a business must be based. He says the best way to tell people what you do is to simplify how you will resolve your client's pain. It's broken down as follows:

I help ... (your niche)

Get ... (their desire)

Without ... (their pain)

By ... (hiring your services or buying your product)

Here is the Film Festival Doctor's 'killer problem statement':

I help: independent filmmakers...

Get: their films into film festivals so they can get the exposure and win the awards they dream about...

Without: submitting their film to the wrong festivals, wasting their money and for the film never to be seen and get the global recognition that it deserves...

By: hiring me as their film festival strategist.

Ed stressed to me the importance of using the phrase 'so they can' in your statement as it shows how you can fix their problem using (1) your methodology, (2) your knowledge and (3) your expertise. And it once again proves to them that you are the leader of your niche.

I use a variation of Ed's 'so they can' technique in the 'About' sections on my websites. For example, the 'About' page on The Film Festival Doctor's website says:

"We help you both save money and make money as a filmmaker – this is achieved via:

Building new business relationships **so you can** create more work for yourself.

Finding a suitable sales agent to sell your film **so you can** get a return on investment

Lobbying your film to our film festival programmer contacts **so you can** get the results you want."

...

Now comes the final part, the Big Domino Statement, which will have a strong impact and make an impression on your prospective clients as well as close business deals and build a loyal following.

The All-Important Big Domino Statement

The Big Domino Statement was originally created by marketing strategist Dan Kennedy and, I believe, popularized by online marketing expert and coach Russell Brunson. Ed has helped me use it and apply it to my business. It's great for helping you build confidence in yourself and your business, which will also help you demonstrate to others that you are the leader of your niche.

The Big Domino Statement is broken down as follows:

If I can make (your market) **believe**

That the only way to get (their desire)

Is through (your method)

The only way to execute (your method) **is by buying my product or service.**

Then all objections become irrelevant and they must invest.

I'm so excited to know what yours is!

Here's the Film Festival Doctor's Big Domino Statement:

If I can make filmmakers (my market) believe the only way to get their film into the right film festivals, win the right awards that grow their career and get their film seen by the right people (desire) is by creating a strategy for their film which is streamlined and focused upon the most suitable festivals to achieve their goals and get the results they want (my method), the only way to do that is by hiring me as their long-term consultant. Then all their fears become irrelevant and they must invest.

...

There will come a time when you'll notice hindsight is indeed a wonderful thing, as I do wish I'd had all these tools earlier in my career when I was setting up my company. However, I'm glad I have them in my tool box now as if I didn't, I wouldn't have been able to introduce you to Ed, his company the Champion Academy, and his techniques, which can help you get your business off the ground.

There was a time during 2011-2012 when I made a huge and embarrassing business mistake. I thought I had found another service I could offer my clients. However, I didn't have the knowledge, experience and skills to resolve their pain for this particular problem. Interestingly, the aftermath of this epic fail gave me the knowledge and skills to create one of the most popular and successful services I now offer my clients...

Exercises to Help You Become the Leader of Your Niche...

1. Using Ed's 'pick your niche' technique, what laser-focused aspects of this niche are you an expert in?

2. Using Ed's technique to figure out if your niche works, is there a market for your niche?

3. How will you solve your clients' problems? To answer this question, try using Ed's 'killer problem statement' (I help/get/without/by).

4. What is your Big Domino Statement? Use the technique Ed taught me to help you figure out yours.

NOTES

3
HOW AN EPIC FAIL CAN BECOME ONE OF YOUR MOST SUCCESSFUL SERVICES

This chapter has a big message contained within it – when a job you are doing feels like horrendously hard work and you are not enjoying it to the point where it is becoming a problem to your wellbeing, stop and go back to what you should be doing; get yourself back in alignment with your soul purpose.

As you are aware by now, I work within the world of film distribution. Film distribution means getting films seen, and in my case it's with regards to film festivals. I am often referred to as a 'film festival agent'. Film distribution also refers to buying and selling films, and sales agents are the type of people who do this job. A sales agent is a person (or a company) who has solid relationships with film distributors. Distribution companies buy films and then screen them digitally on television or theatrically in a cinema. For example, Netflix and iTunes are both film distribution companies.

I thought I had found a way to resolve a persistent and frequently occurring problem for my filmmaker clientele. However, my solution didn't work, and I had to go on a journey of anxiety, stress and defeat which, thankfully, led to me finding an even better solution a few years later.

The Film Sales Agent World

There are a lot more sales agents than there are film festival agents; in fact, there are hundreds of sales agents around the world selling films, so it's certainly not as niche as The Film Festival Doctor. Almost every filmmaker is aware of what a sales agent is and what they do. Filmmakers are very keen to find a sales agent as they often need to pay back their film's investor(s) through selling the film around the world.

A sales agent will share the money they receive from the distribution companies with the producer of the film. The film sales market is a crowded place and in order for a sales agent to really stand out they need to have very good quality films for sale; however, they also need to be the kind of films that distributors will pay money for. Sales agents tend to specialize in selling a particular genre of film – for example, horror movies, documentaries, art house films, faith and spirituality films, children's films etc.

Almost all my clients, who had produced independent feature films, told me they were anxious to find the right sales agent as they wanted (a) their film seen on other platforms besides film festivals and (b) to make some kind of profit on the film, no matter how small.

There are a handful of film festivals – Berlinale, Cannes, Sundance, Toronto International Film Festival, Filmmart and the American Film Market (AFM) – that also have a film market. This is where buyers and sellers meet to close deals to buy films.

Sales companies attend the film market and hire a sales booth to sell the films they are currently representing to distribution companies. Sales agents have endless tiring meetings, lunches and dinners with distributors in order to close as many lucrative deals as possible.

Film markets are all about the business of film. They are the place where, potentially, sales agents can make a lot of money. The film market has changed dramatically for sales agents selling independent films as the prices have decreased; however, there is still money to be made selling one film all around the world for a lower price.

Film markets are different to film festivals in that they are literally markets where business deals are signed. There's no dress code, no red carpet, no champagne and canapes, and no getting glammed up to watch a film premiere; all this takes place at a film festival. However, with the exception of Film Mart and AFM, all film markets take place within film festivals, so it was, therefore, a great place for me to make connections, especially with distribution companies.

When I attended Berlinale and Cannes, I got to know a few distributors who were looking for films to buy that were screening in competition at these bigger film festivals. It suddenly occurred to me that I could offer my clients an additional service – selling their film to distributors and helping them get a return on investment for their financiers. I created a separate company, The Film Sales Doctor, which operated exactly like a sales agency.

I wasn't planning on hiring a booth and becoming a full-service agent. Instead, I made it clear to my clients that this was a lower key service where I would manage them at the film festivals but also have meetings with buyers on their behalf at the festival markets.

The Film Festival Doctor had started to make a name for itself within the independent film world and John (the man I met during my first Cannes Film Festival trip in 2010) and I had become extremely close colleagues. I trusted him as my business advisor and asked if he would come on board as an integral part of the Film Sales Doctor and help me close deals with distribution companies. He agreed to work on a commission-based deal and, as always, was there to support me.

At the time when John joined The Film Sales Doctor, he was still working as a full-time producer on a slate of films. John now runs his own very successful sales company, specializing in low budget action, thriller and horror that sells well internationally. He knows the film sales arena inside out and always attends the major film markets with the films he is representing. He also produces his own films with his team and sells them through his company.

The most – and only! – successful sales deal that The Film Sales Doctor closed was for a documentary feature film called *Tibet Meditation*...

The Journey to Sell *Tibet Meditation*

I realized after I agreed to sell *Tibet Meditation* that I'd made a big mistake in not changing my business model. Up until then, all the films The Film Sales Doctor represented were festival films that were travelling the circuit and looking to get sold and distributed. *Tibet Meditation* came to my attention after I met the filmmaker at a networking event and it was by no means a festival film; it was a documentary more suited to a TV audience. In addition, the filmmaker was focused mainly on selling the film rather than having it seen at film festivals. However, I was so determined to make this new venture work that I decided to take it on and focus solely upon finding a buyer for it. After many long conversations, he agreed to sign the contract for me to sell it.

I had no documentary distribution contacts at all, but I was determined to find some! By chance, I met a documentary distributor at a restaurant during the Berlinale Film Festival. They were from a well-known company and mentioned that they had a catalogue focused on faith and spirituality films. Aha! "I have the perfect film for you!" I said. I knew that *Tibet Meditation* was a perfect fit. I pitched it to them, and they gave me their business card. After a lot of follow up, they made an offer. It was a low price, but it was a good first deal, and hopefully the first of many for this film.

John and I closed the deal together during the Cannes Film Festival a few months later. John asked all the right questions regarding how they would transfer payment, what the terms were, what materials they needed from us etc. It took a long time to close the deal as the contract was huge and a lot of time was spent going back and forth on the agreement to check it was legitimate (which it was, thankfully). I was also extra thorough during this process as I didn't want to miss anything important. The filmmaker had to get music clearances before we could proceed, otherwise he would be in a lot of legal trouble, and this inevitably took time. Eventually he did get everything sorted and the film was soon available to buy.

Looking back on this experience, I realize I had no idea how to close a sales deal and absolutely no experience within this area of the film business whatsoever. The more time I spent within this world, the more I learnt that it was a very tricky part of the industry to navigate. There were no hard and fast rules; you just needed a lot of experience of negotiation and closing deals to get a decent one. I had no idea what you needed to be careful of or what the process involved from start to finish. I didn't even know what 'film sales deliverables' were. I naively assumed they would want the same materials we gave film festivals but no, far from it; they wanted a lot of different things that the filmmaker was expected to pay for – and sometimes they couldn't afford it. I was grateful for John's support and he was always available; however, it was during a meeting a few months later that I realized I had a lot to learn about working as a sales agent. I couldn't do this by myself and it wasn't even something I was actually capable of doing anymore.

That Unforgettably Horrendous Meeting

The moment I realized I was in too deep and completely out of my depth was when I had a meeting with two prospective filmmakers at a cafe in Soho, London. John had been delayed in meetings and wasn't able to join me; however, he said to relay all the questions they had back to him, and he'd help me out. When we were discussing the sales strategy and how I would sell their film I realized I didn't know what I was doing; I did not know which distribution companies I was going to approach or how I would pitch it to them. They had already spoken to several more experienced agents with strong ideas on marketing, pitching and positioning within the market. And when they asked me: "Which distributors do you have solid connections with?" that made me realize I did not have the key ingredient that is the backbone of every film sales company – a plethora of strong connections and solid relationships with film distribution companies and their buyers.

In all honesty, their question made me realize that although I had many, many film festival programmer contacts, I only knew a handful of distributors. I didn't have enough contacts to run The

Film Sales Doctor business. Most importantly, although I had closed a sales deal it hadn't been enough to fully resolve the client's pain or make a sufficient profit for them and their investors. John always said I would be a good sales agent as I knew how to look after the filmmakers, was committed to the job and had the best intention and energy behind me, and he was happy to provide support and advice behind the scenes. But as much as that sounded like a winning combination, it wouldn't work without the key contacts.

I left that meeting feeling like a fraud. It was the first time in my life that I cried myself to sleep through sheer embarrassment. I had failed. The following morning, I decided to not pursue The Film Sales Doctor venture any further. Instead, I went straight back to focusing on nurturing my Film Festival Doctor business and doing what I was born to do.

It wasn't until a few years later at the Berlin Film Festival (which is indeed the same place where I met the distributors of *Tibet Meditation* – clearly that festival is good for networking!) that I came to realize the value of that epic fail. Although it was stressful, the experience helped me to identify another gap in the market and, simultaneously, solve the problem I was trying to resolve several years earlier via The Film Sales Doctor company.

Mr Magician Billy

I met Billy Hurman at the Berlin Film Festival in 2017. At the time he was working as a sales agent for a UK-based film sales company. Billy has an incredible portfolio and has certainly had a sparkling film career! With over 30 years' experience in the film industry, he has attended nearly every major film festival in the world and worked at both *The Hollywood Reporter* and *Screen*

International, two of the biggest film industry trade publications. He has also dabbled in production; he co-wrote and produced a feature film called *The Sea Change,* which was selected for The Sundance Festival in the late 1990s. Billy has also been a board director for a PLC media company where he worked as a film sales agent, representing over 100 films across all budget ranges over the last 20 years.

Obviously the more I began to bond with Billy the more I recognized that he was extremely knowledgeable and knew a lot of film sales agents and film distributors around the world. We re-connected a few months after we initially met at an event I co-created and co-hosted with a colleague of mine called The Essex Film Creatives Club. This was a networking event for filmmakers and film creatives based in the county of Essex in the UK. When I first moved to Essex, I noticed there were very few networking events for Essex-based filmmakers within the county; they had to travel into London to connect with like-minded people. Southend-on-Sea had a huge talent hub that I wanted to tap into, as I was keen to set up a film community within Essex, network with more filmmakers and also give other Essex creatives the opportunity to connect with each other. The awesome Paul Cotgrove, who is the founder and director of the brilliant Southend-on-Sea Film Festival and who I'm good friends with, knew exactly where to host it and how to promote it. It is a great success and lots of people connected who then eventually made films together, which I inevitably ended up distributing into film festivals!

Billy lives close to the event with his beautiful wife, Alex, and their gorgeous, lively dog, Bonham. One month they attended the Essex Film Creatives Club event and Billy informed me he had left the sales company he was working for and launched his own consultancy business, which involved him helping filmmakers to find a suitable sales agent for their film.

In a nutshell, a filmmaker with a completed film would approach him looking to attach a sales agent to it so it could be sold to distribution companies around the world. Billy aspires to resolve their pain by finding the right sales agent for their film. Many filmmakers do not have the contacts or the relationships that he has with sales agents, therefore Billy can make suggestions and match them with suitable sales agencies.

The penny dropped and I had an 'aha' moment – he could possibly resolve that pain for those of my clients who were looking for a sales agent. He has a great deal of experience within this area, plus he has built up many connections over the years. He would propose a strategic plan to the producers, which outlined how he would work to try and attach a sales agent.

Billy has a 100% success rate and I felt he gave five-star customer service to his clients in exactly the way I did. I really wanted him to be a part of my team: he was the missing ingredient. He agreed to join The Festival Film Doctor team and has been working ever since to attach sales agents to my clients' films.

A Team to Be Proud Of

My favorite success story of working with Billy was when we represented a film made in South Africa called *Kanarie*.

Kanarie is a gem of a film. It's a coming-of-age LGBTQ war musical about a small-town boy who gets chosen to serve his compulsory two-year military training in the South African Defence Force Choir and Concert group – known as the Canaries – during the height of the apartheid regime. The film is fresh, innovative and has an amazing opening sequence to rival the Oscar-winning *La La Land.* Although it might not sound like it from the synopsis, it's actually a film that can travel outside of South Africa; it is accessible to film audiences over the world.

The producers of the film wanted to find a sales agent to sell it and also get it seen at festivals around the world. They had no contacts or experience within these areas and were recommended to me by colleagues. Billy found them a sales agent he felt would be a perfect fit for their film, a company called Breaking Glass Entertainment that specialized in selling LGBTQ films. They took *Kanarie* to film markets, promoted it well to their buyer contacts and it made its investor money back very quickly. The film dominated the festival circuit and was screened at over 40 film festivals around the world, including all the key LGBTQ festivals as well as several top tier festivals that were not LGBTQ-specific, including the Molodist Film Festival in the Ukraine and the Costa Rica International Film Festival. It also won 13 awards, many of which were for Best Film. I'm so pleased that I'd partnered with Billy and The Film Sales Doctor episode was behind me by the time I met these clients.

Billy is a valuable asset to my company, and we love working with him; not only is he hilarious but Billy, Alex and Bonham have become wonderful friends. I'm so pleased we have this bond and that he approaches working with a client with the same mindset and attitude that I do – which includes always going the extra mile, thinking outside the box and listening to our clients.

I make it very clear to our clients that we will work diligently for them to try and attach a suitable sales agent for their film and that Billy is the person who will work very hard on the producer's behalf to that end. I also make it very clear that we are *not* a film sales agency and that we *do not* sell films on behalf of our clients. That is firmly in the past.

Working with Billy taught me the importance of delegation; a valuable lesson and golden rule I learnt from the Film Sales Doctor experience is that you can't do everything yourself, and neither will you be able to deliver quality results alone. I will never forget what Ed J C Smith told me when I was feeling overwhelmed whilst trying to make The Film Sales Doctor work: "How will you be able to grow your business if you are doing everything by yourself?" From then on, delegation became a priority.

I am very grateful to work with a dream team. The longest serving and most senior project manager on my team is Victoria; she's been with me for many years and has the same ethics, dedication and commitment as me. She always gives 110% and is thorough – these are qualities all your staff should have. Her job involves talking to our film festival contacts with me, pitching the films, submitting them to film festivals, organizing festival screenings and sorting out the deliverables.

No doubt she's reading this and will be pleased to know that she has a job here with me for life! The same also applies to my other key team members, especially Nicole, who does a marvelous job managing events with me and promoting The Film Festival Doctor to her network of contacts. Nicole has believed in me and the business since day one and she is an incredible spiritual force of nature who always inspires me. In fact, she created an additional service that my company now offers, The First Time Filmmaker Package, which is very popular with student filmmakers. My consultant Shelagh has encyclopedic knowledge of the festival circuit and I love working with her to put together a film festival strategy; we co-create the magic for our clients. Billy is obviously indispensable, and Domenico looks after our clients wonderfully. I always support my team with kindness and generosity, and I love supporting them whenever they need my assistance.

It is essential to have an accountant and a lawyer as part of your team. Delegating this nature of work is crucial as anything to do with accounting and legal issues requires knowledge and experience that can't be acquired by researching on Google. These types of people might charge a lot but what they do is essential for your business and will remove a huge weight from your mind as well as decrease stress levels.

So far, you've learnt how to discover your soul purpose, which will guide you to find your specific niche, how to talk about your niche to other people and, in this chapter, how to stick to your niche and avoid those roles you were not born to do. Another important aspect of a business is your logo and branding, as this also needs to be in alignment with your soul purpose in order to attract potential clients who will trust that you can solve their problem.

Exercises to Help You Become the Leader of Your Niche...

1. What does your client not need help with that, therefore, you do not need to include in your services?

2. Who could you delegate work to?

3. What types of jobs would you create for your team?

4. What qualities will your ideal work colleagues possess, and what will you be looking for when hiring them? (i.e. good time management skills, excellent problem-solving skills, dedication to the job etc.)

NOTES

4
WHY ENERGETIC BRANDING IS IMPORTANT FOR YOU AND YOUR BUSINESS

I will never forget a very important piece of advice my colleague Colin gave me during the Abertoir Horror Festival back in 2010, when I was sharing with him my ideas for the Film Festival Doctor business. He said: "The most important thing for any company is having a strong and striking logo and website – if you don't have either of these or they're not any good then no one will want to come into the shop."

That was spot on! After he said that, I started looking at the logos and websites of my favorite brands, which were three clothing companies: Bella Sorella (I always wear loads of their clothes to film festivals), Silk Fred (another company whose clothes I always wear to film festivals) and BlueBella, a lingerie company. I loved their logos and made a note of the reasons I felt drawn to them. The colors and fonts used by these brands cultivated feelings of connection with the company and excitement about their products, and when I received emails from them showcasing their new range of clothing, I felt the quality of their products would be high and I would be safe buying from them. The products lived up to my expectations and their customer service got five stars.

This was exactly what I wanted my logo and website to convey. I wanted people to feel they could rely on my brand to look after them and their film; I wanted to evoke feelings of warmth and trust. It is always important to show your clientele that your business is a brand that will always deliver on its promises.

This is the first chapter that discusses how to integrate spiritual practices into your business. Chapters 7-9 discuss in more detail how to use spiritual techniques (including cosmic ordering, manifestations and vision boards) in your daily working life. This chapter emphasizes the importance of why your branding needs to be of the energetic kind – this is different to standard branding, which doesn't take energy into account, as you'll soon see. We will also look at why it is important to use and wear specific colors to help your soul purpose shine and attract the right type of clientele.

The Reason Why My Logo Had to Feature a Woman

I was very focused on making it clear to the world that my company was founded and run by a woman – especially because many people assumed it was run by a man since it had the word 'doctor' in it, and the film industry is also a male dominated environment. I wanted to make it clear that this is who I am and this is my identity – I am a female entrepreneur working in the film industry as The Film Festival Doctor.

As the years went by The Film Festival Doctor became a part of my identity, and my logo helped to generate interest. My brand became more established within the independent film community via the support and success we were delivering for our clients and when I attended networking events and film festivals I was referred to as 'The Film Festival Doctor' or 'The Film Doctor' rather than Rebekah. People started to recognize I was 110% committed to my business, my niche and my clients.

On my website and social media channels I positioned myself as the face of the company. My Facebook, Instagram and LinkedIn profile pictures all use the same headshot of me, so the branding is consistent and people recognize the brand. Photos taken at film festivals also raise awareness of my brand and show how I support my clients on their journey touring the circuit.

The 'About' section on The Film Festival Doctor's website has three sections: 'About', 'The Team', and 'Dr Rebekah Louisa'. I was advised to create a page that focused exclusively on me, the founder of the company, as this can help build trust with the client. When people visit your website, they will learn more about you and your story, and this will help you to build rapport with them. In addition, presenting yourself in this way on your website will also help you to stand out as the leader of your niche. My story on the 'Dr Rebekah Louisa' page of my website is honest and engaging; I discuss why I changed my career from academia to the world of film, I demonstrate my commitment towards getting results for my clients and I share a sample of those results. There is also a link to an interview I did for *The Success Story* podcast, so people can hear my story in more detail.

Back to Colin's valid point about branding at the beginning of this chapter ... Colin's graphic designer colleague Phil created a logo for me, and I loved it. It really stood out, it was simple yet effective and it was different. He used a font I had never heard of called Caviar Dreams, which really worked. I loved the 70s-style image of the woman, with her immaculate afro hair standing out alongside film reel earrings, 35mm film winding across her head. What Phil created was iconic. The image of this woman and my brand is now widely recognized across the independent film industry and certainly encourages people to take a closer look at the company when they notice it online and on my promotional materials. My brand slogan (in other words, the promise) is "Your Partner for Successful Exposure Worldwide", which we never fail to achieve; we always deliver on our promises.

However, when I met Marie Diamond, Feng Shui master and contributor to the very popular self-help book *The Secret* (written by Rhonda Byrne) in 2013, she pointed out that my logo was actually blocking me from attracting more clients, sales and success because the energy of the logo was not flowing in the right direction...

Marie Diamond's Feng Shui Infused Magic

Marie and I met at a networking event in London through our mutual and dear friend Phil. If it wasn't for Phil taking the time to introduce us my business would be nowhere near as successful as it is now, therefore I will always be grateful for his kindness in connecting me with her. Marie is my go-to person when it comes to working on the energetic branding of my company.

Marie's track record is simply breathtaking, and she is an exemplary example of being the leader in her niche of Feng Shui. Feng Shui literally translates from Chinese as 'wind' (feng) and 'water' (shui). It's the art of arranging buildings, objects, spaces and life to achieve harmony and balance. Marie talks about Feng Shui in the infamous book *The Secret*, which explores the law of attraction and shows you how to attract more success and happiness into your life. For the last 25 years, Marie has been the spiritual mentor and Feng Shui master for hundreds of thousands of students worldwide, including top public speakers, international best-selling authors, celebrities in the music and movie industries, politicians and top athletes. She has become a global household name in her field. In addition to doing one-to-one consultancy and adding Feng Shui cures to people's homes, she offers courses and products to people who are looking to heal their lives and work with the law of attraction.

During this networking event she looked at the logo on my business card and said it was dull; it was projecting a low vibration, it had no pull towards it, and it wasn't allowing my soul purpose to shine. In fact, it was not showing what I could do for my clients.

Marie explained that it needed more color; it was far too dark and there was too much black within it. She also pointed out that, most importantly, the woman in the image had a huge energy blocking problem as she was looking away from the name of my company, whereas she should have been looking in directly at it. She literally had her back to it and Marie said that in Feng Shui terms that means you have your back towards your clients; you're not facing them or welcoming them to your brand (or your shop, as Colin would say). How could they trust your brand if you were not engaging with them? It was almost as if I was subconsciously not allowing my soul purpose to emerge. I had given up before I had even started.

The next day, following Marie's guidance, I asked Phil to tweak the logo.

When Phil made the changes to the logo the energy changed dramatically. By turning the woman's head to look directly at the name of my company she instantly feels and looks so much more connected to the brand; she is literally welcoming people into my 'shop'. She is in alignment with our clients and is ready to start talking to them. Marie suggested we make the words 'Film Festival' red to represent the red carpet at film festivals and events. She told me that red represents balance and harmony with regards to relationships and this meant I'd be able to cultivate solid and trustworthy relationships with my clients. Marie explained that the balance that red represents can help me to make good decisions when weighing up options, or balance intense energies or activities within the company. Visit my website www.thefilmfestivaldoctor.com to view the logo.

Not only did Marie change the energy of my logo and the brand, she helped me to change the energy in myself too. During our first consultancy together after we changed the logo, she mentioned that I was thinking too small. I explained that I was feeling depressed about not closing deals with the clients I wanted to work with, as they were all saying they had no budget or couldn't afford my services. I was beginning to wonder if filmmakers would be able to afford my consultancy rate. Perhaps I was charging too much? In fact, the opposite was true: I was charging too little. Marie assured me there were plenty of filmmakers and film production companies around the world who could afford my services. I needed to stop thinking small in order to attract the right type of clientele to my company. Marie was right; there was an abundance of them. My problem was that I was thinking far too small and also engaging with too many limiting beliefs revolving around lack, specifically lack of money and clients.

Another thing Marie said was contributing to this issue was the dull colors I wore. She had noticed that I wore lots of black, grey and dark purple, and these weren't the right colors to attract clients towards me. She said I looked too much like the design of my old logo and I needed to raise my vibration and energy. And she knew exactly how to change that.

Marie's Quantum Colors Technique

During my consultation with Marie, she used her Quantum Colors Technique to help lift the energy of my mental health so I could think bigger and attract the right type of clientele. In her Diamond Quantum Colors course, Marie explains that everything in the universe is alive with energy. She teaches how to use specific colors to more easily manifest greater success, health, relationships, and wisdom in your life.

When we met, I was wearing a black dress and white cardigan. Marie said I needed to wear more saffron yellow, gold, rose and pink. At first, I wasn't convinced, as I didn't think those colors would suit me. However, when she told me why, it made sense for me to trust her advice and invest in some new clothing. Marie explained that wearing saffron yellow would help to activate compassion when I chose to show trust, patience and kindness towards my clients. It would also help me to listen to advice, create a gentle ease of love and support, and feel more compassion for myself. Gold, she told me, would help to activate abundance when I wanted to increase financial growth, achieve greater results from work and investments, and manifest the results I wanted for myself and my clients. The color rose would help to activate love when I wanted to be more open and outgoing, receive support, or establish or improve significant relationships, including romantic partners, friends, family, and business associates. Pink would also activate tenderness when I chose to be gentle or when I wanted to receive tender and loving attention; it would stimulate my senses, and express appreciation and sweetness.

This might sound a bit bonkers and I'll admit it took me a while to get my head around her quantum colors methodology. However, throughout our meeting, I noticed that Marie looked incredible – she literally shone like a diamond. Her clothes all blended together harmoniously and she had a very striking presence, which was enhanced by the colors of her clothes all energetically binding together. We'd met in a restaurant in Soho, London and I noticed that all eyes were on her, as she was so striking and eye catching. It was at that point that I knew wearing brighter colors would really help me, so I took her advice and began to change my wardrobe. And my goodness, she was right – my mental health and business changed instantly!

I went from wearing dark colors to bright pastel shades. I also mixed them together to create a very distinctive and striking look. My mental state shifted from only wanting to wear black and grey to not allowing any of those colors into my wardrobe and only allowing in bright colors and sexy dresses. I didn't want to come across as the kind of person who was living in the shadows. Marie taught me that in order to be the leader of your niche, you need to be bold and stand out – not just via your branding but also through the way you present yourself to the world.

If you turn to the front cover of this book, you'll see I'm wearing a black dress with gold spots all over it, and a gold flower necklace. The impression my outfit creates would be very different if that dress was just black and had no abundant colors surrounding my energy field. When I posted that picture on my social media channels, people commented on how strong and beautiful I looked. The photo demonstrates what Marie taught me: a positive mind set + wearing the right colors = an endless flow of abundance.

When I wore gold necklaces and gold-colored clothing, I felt a sense of authority and financial freedom. I really did feel like I was running the show and I was finally allowing my soul purpose to shine on the outside. I felt like I did not need to rely on anyone else, either; I knew how to stand my ground. I always wore gold when I attended business meetings to show I was focused on the world of business. When I met Marie, I had lovely blonde highlights in my hair; however, my hairdresser encouraged me to take the plunge and dye it. He suggested that we go for a golden blonde shade, which he created especially for me, and it looked stunning. I loved my hair color and it helped me to feel abundant and rich in health, wealth and happiness as soon as I woke up each day.

I always wear saffron yellow when I meet my clients for the first time in order to begin the process of building our bond. This color also tends to be my go-to nail varnish choice so I can be compassionate to everyone, including myself. I wore rose and pink when I was at events and when I was hanging out with industry friends, as this proved to be a really good color combination to wear to help activate my communication levels. There is a lot of pink in my house and office; this color certainly helps to stimulate my senses and inspiration. When I begin working with a new client, all my ideas and inspiration flow to me when I'm in my office, which is covered in pink. Whenever my dear friend Holly visits, she says it feels like she is "walking on a cloud," as it's so calming.

I also noticed that as soon as I switched to wearing these colors, people around me began to look at me differently. I was radiating positivity, excitement and joy – I was in alignment with my soul purpose and I was feeling a lot more balanced, both mentally and physically. My energy was positive, both on the inside and the outside. This brightened up the energy of the brand when people met me, and they never forgot me when they saw me. I was often referred to as looking 'distinctive' and that I 'really stand out'. These were such lovely compliments as they helped me to feel that I was the leader of my niche and the face of my brand.

I always receive positive comments on my logo now that the energy of it has shifted and it has become bolder, bigger, better and brighter. With my new mindset I attract the type of clientele who have the budgets to work with me, and when I wear clothes that lift my energy field, I feel harmonious. I love how, despite the tweaks, we kept the general essence of the logo Phil created, as it still builds that trust with my clients that is so important to me.

...

As previously discussed, discovering your 'why', being able to find your niche and make it work, articulating what you do to your prospective clients, knowing what services your clients want and ensuring your branding is of the energetic kind are all extremely important elements when you start your first business and become a leader of your niche.

The next step is to ensure your company has a watertight infrastructure and systems in place before you begin. My company didn't have this until I met Gerlanda Milito, who quickly knocked it into shape, which helped even more abundance flow towards me and my business...

Exercises to Help You Become the Leader of Your Niche...

1. What do you want your company logo to look like? Start sketching some ideas and make a list of the fonts you like.

2. What will your company website look like? Start making a list of some of your favorite websites and the qualities you like about them.

3. What will be your brand promise?

4. What techniques will you implement to become the face of your brand?

5. What colors are important for you to wear on a daily basis and also when you start running your business?

NOTES

5
HOW TO ORGANIZE YOUR BUSINESS AND POSITION YOURSELF AS AN EXPERT

I've spoken a lot in the previous chapters about the people who have been (and will always be) important to my business. The next two chapters are dedicated to another person who is more than a valuable asset to my company. That woman is business strategist Gerlanda Milioto.

Gerlanda is the kind of person you wish you met on the day you started your business. Her LinkedIn profile is outstanding and, as with Marie Diamond, she is a leader of her niche. She describes herself as a "dynamic leader with extensive experience in business development, strategic partnership, recruitment and selection." She does indeed have a huge success rate within these areas; she has a strong track record of helping start-up companies achieve their business objectives and has helped them make millions.

The great thing about running your business and immersing yourself in your work is that you're doing what your soul purpose is guiding you to do, since you are, after all, born to do it. This is the fun part. However, what is also very important to remember is that your business needs to have organized systems in place so it can make money, grow and expand over time. If you don't have any systems in place, your business will not work. It is important to always keep an eye on what is working and what needs changing so you can continue to do what you love (and what you are supposed to be doing) forever and remain a leader in your business niche.

During this chapter I interview Gerlanda and we discuss how to implement a water-tight infrastructure in your business. First, I will share with you the story of how I met Gerlanda and why I'm so pleased that I chose to attend the worst networking event in the world...

The Best and Worst Networking Event Experience

I met Gerlanda at what started out to be a horrendously boring and dull networking event, a London Business Owners mixer event for entrepreneurs. It was the type of event you are not sure about attending as it could be hit or miss in terms of who you meet and the overall quality of the event. Part of me thought it was worthwhile going, as there would be plenty of people from different industries, including the creative sector – I thought there might be some people from the film business attending who would be worth connecting with. However, as it was so broad I knew there might not be any useful contacts at all, since not everyone you meet will be a valuable connection. The main reason I went was because my friend Claudia was keen for us to go and have a night out in central London and she can *always* brighten up a dull event with her fun energy – so for that reason I was sold.

The moral of this story is that you never know who you are going to meet – you've probably heard this a million times before but it's true. The event started out a bit strangely as there were lots of people there who only had vague ideas about businesses they *might* start. However, although I didn't meet a single filmmaker that night, I did meet someone who (in addition to Ed J C Smith) helped me to radically change my business and increase my turnover to $20K a month.

During the event, Gerlanda gave an amazing presentation that clearly defined exactly what she does and how she can help a business grow and become more successful. I spoke with her for a long time afterwards and followed up with her the next day. Later, we spoke on the phone and she told me what was missing from my company: infrastructure. I had spent the first couple of years running my business with what I thought was an organized system. However, Gerlanda soon made me realize that my main problem was the 'back end' of my accounting system: it was nowhere near as organized as it should be! I needed to create a pipeline and monthly key performance indicators (KPIs), and I also needed to position myself as an expert to my clientele. I thought I was doing well closing deals, but it turned out I really needed to refine my sales pitch so I could work with more clients.

What are the secrets to achieving that? Read on and Gerlanda will reveal everything you need to know!

What Is A Sales Pipeline?

The first essential component you will need to implement within your company infrastructure is a sales pipeline. But what is a sales pipeline?

Gerlanda: *"A sales pipeline is an organized, visual way of tracking multiple potential buyers as they progress through different stages in the purchasing process. It is a way to keep a record of the amount of business a company expects to receive in the coming weeks, months or years. Typically, it is used when companies have multiple leads to show when these leads become either confirmed sales or lost opportunities. In short, it is a snapshot of where prospects are in the sales process.*

A sales pipeline also shows how close a prospect is to reaching the close of a sale. It shows what the seller is doing during the entire sales process to ensure that prospective business turns into a business opportunity: how long it takes for a specific prospect to be secured into a sale and what may be causing the delay. It is also used to track the time it takes between the placement of orders and when the goods or services are actually delivered."

I love my sales pipeline. I monitor and update it every day. Each morning I look at what film projects I have in the pipeline and the status of each one, and I make notes on the status of each lead. For example, if I sent brochures to a client and requested a follow up call four days ago then I'll reach out again to see if they would like to schedule a call the following week and also to get an update on what is happening and where they are at. If I don't hear from them, I move them to the non-priority section of the pipeline. If I hear from them, schedule a call and they become a client then that's great. If not, they remain in the non-priority section. I always continue to monitor this part of the pipeline and I keep in touch with them, building the relationship every single time. I never delete them as sometimes a cold/dead lead can become a warm lead if they get back in touch, either with a new film or because they want to continue the conversation now they know what their goals are and what they want to achieve.

I would advise you to set up your pipeline using an Excel

spreadsheet and create the following columns:

- name of client
- date you connected with the client
- the service/product they are interested in
- status (so you can keep a note of when you last communicated with them and where you are at in terms of closing a deal with them)
- type of lead
- cost of the service
- the prospective client's contact details

You'll find the status column is the one you will update the most as you make progress towards closing deals with your clients. In the 'type of lead' section you can mark them as a 'hot lead', meaning you're coming close to making a deal; a 'warm lead', meaning this person has the potential to become a client; and a 'cold lead', meaning there's not a huge amount of potential yet or you have not heard from them. I'd also separate the pipeline into two different sections – 'priority', where you put the deals you are close to closing (so all your hot and warm leads), and 'non-priority', for the ones who have gone cold.

What is a KPI?

The second essential component you will need to implement within your company's infrastructure is a KPI. Back to Gerlanda for an explanation.

Gerlanda: "*KPI stands for Key Performance Indicator and is used to keep track of where business is coming from as well as where you expect it to come from in the future. It's a way of measuring your company's performance. For example, you may have multiple channels where business could come from, such as:*

- *Your website*
- *Social media*
    - *Facebook*
    - *Instagram*
    - *Industry-related forums*
    - *LinkedIn*
- *Events you attend*
    - *National events*
    - *International events*
- *Workshops you attend*
- *Events you may organize*
- *Word of mouth*
    - *Direct referrals - from people who know you or past/existing clients of yours*
    - *Direct recommendations - as above*
    - *Strategic partnerships - companies who refer business to you from their own clients in cases where they may not be able to offer your type of service to their clients and they would therefore pass them onto you for a percentage of the sale or for commission. In addition, you may want to organize joint events. That way, it will help you build a good relationship with your clients as well as their clients.*
    - *Affiliate websites - other companies related to your industry with whom you have formed an agreement where you have a presence on each other's website. Anyone clicking on a specific advert on their website will be directed to your website and vice versa. Alternatively, the affiliate may close the business on your behalf and give you a percentage of what they sell, for example; a book, workshop or training program you offer, which they sell on your behalf. A third option*

is that they charge you for every click made on your advert that appears on their website."

And Gerlanda, how do you implement the KPI model into your business?

Gerlanda: "*By keeping track of where business is coming from, you can then put in place a KPI forecast by assessing which channel has worked best in bringing in more business, i.e. where you are planning the business to come from and which channel the most sales have come from. This is done by seeing how much business you have closed from a particular channel (e.g. social media and networking events) and allocating more time in implementing marketing strategies in a particular area as well as being able to plan which event(s) or workshops would be more beneficial for you to take time out to attend. You can also see from which social media channel you are getting most business or interest. This is because - always remember - a lead can only be as good as the amount of work you put into your leads, and how active you are with following up and closing the lead, as well as many other sales skills required to secure the business."*

KPIs are really fantastic as they help you identify patterns in which service or product you are selling is performing the best and making the most money. I review mine each month and always keep notes, as these patterns can help you figure out if you need to refine your sales pitch or decide to stop promoting a service that is no longer working.

When I started looking into the world of KPIs with Gerlanda, I noticed that I tend to get more film festival strategy consultancy clients than I do script development consultancy clients, as the former is what we are more well known for. In addition, all my social media images and posts are connected to film festivals, therefore this is another reason why I receive more business for this particular service. I still like offering the script consultancy service, as I tend to get one or two clients a month and those clients are all via referrals from other clients. Although demand for script consultancy isn't as high as for the other consultancy services I offer, it's still great that there is a small yet committed client base for it.

What is a Budget Forecast?

The third essential component you will need to implement is a budget forecast. But what is a budget forecast?

Gerlanda: "*A budget forecast sets targets for income and expenditure so you can hold yourself accountable to those targets as the year progresses. It is a visibility tool, where you can indicate your goals and ambitions for your business, and it is a useful tool to show figures for what you are planning in the next one, two or even three years, on a monthly basis. Whereas the KPI tracks where the business is coming from and helps you plan where business could be coming from, the budget forecast is the financial side of your business and is used to plan ahead, to plan where growth could take place and to see if you are on track by comparing what you planned for the financial side of your business in any particular month to what was actually accomplished.*"

And how do you implement a budget forecast into your business?

Gerlanda: "*A budget forecast should be put in place alongside the KPI reports.*

Budget Forecasts are divided into four main sections:

(i) *Sales - money coming into your business (or investment gone into your business, e.g. loans, grants etc.)*
(ii) *Expenses - money going out of your business, e.g. costs such as travel, office expenses, production costs, wages etc.*
(iii) *Cash Flow - this will show you how much money you have in the bank on a monthly basis (or how much you forecast to have in the bank) once sales are taken into consideration minus expenses for a particular month or year. It is the available money you have to use for the following month(s) to put back into your business.*
(iv) *Profit and Loss (better known as P&L). By taking your expenses away from your sales, you will know how much net profit you have made or aim to make for a particular period.*

Budget forecasts should include realistic figures. One should always take the worst-case scenario into consideration as, if your performance is better for one particular month, you can then make changes to that particular month including your actuals and can then see how much more growth you could be making compared to what was originally forecast. It is a fantastic tool for start-ups to help them avoid over-spending, as some people see money in the bank and forget they may have a bad month coming up because of unforeseen circumstances (or the time of the year when business might be slow, for example, the annual Christmas period)."

I couldn't believe that I wasn't budgeting in the way I should have been when I first began running my business. Luckily, I didn't have a huge amount of overheads as I didn't need to buy any machinery or purchase in a huge amount of stock to re-sell. My expenses were mainly wages for me and the contractors who work for me, travel, and food and accommodation when attending festivals. No matter what you do or how big or small your business is, you need to do a budget forecast at the start of each month. Similar to your pipeline, it is important to monitor this each day to ensure you are not overspending and to analyze how much money you are making in terms of sales coming in versus expenses going out. Always ask yourself if you are on target and if not, review your KPI to figure out which channels are working and which aren't. The more energy and time you put into the ones that are working, the more chance you have of meeting your monthly targets.

What is a Sales Forecast?

The fourth essential component you will need to implement within your company infrastructure is a sales forecast. Gerlanda, what is a sales forecast?

Gerlanda: "*A sales forecast is just as the name states, a forecast of your sales across a period of time to help you keep track of how much money you plan to come into your business. It is best used hand in hand with KPIs. Through KPIs, you will forecast how much business (and what type of sales, identifying different products or services you sell) can be made. By forecasting what type of business you plan to bring in on your KPIs, you then convert this financially onto your sales forecast.*

For example, a program you are selling may have three different levels of income so you may want to sell more at one level than the other, e.g. one program may be £3,450 and another may be £2,500, so if you want to achieve an income in the next month of £10,000 you would need to sell at least two programs at £3,450 and one at £2,500 and then possibly make up the difference with a service selling for £600.

Your KPI will show you where it's best to get this new business from by comparing your past performance in the various sales channels so you have an idea of how much business you can forecast to include in your upcoming months."

How do you implement a sales forecast in your business?

Gerlanda: "*Most start-up companies do not know what their income/expenditure may be in the upcoming months or years. However, they know how much they will be charging for their services, what kind of services or products they will be selling and what expenses they will have to pay. So, for a start-up, the first thing is to set themselves a realistic target for the first month and upcoming months. Some prefer to start backwards, looking at the expenses they will have for the first year and then figuring out how much they will need to make in the way of income to be able to either break even or make a profit. Then, divide the annual forecasted/needed income into the twelve months of the year, possibly at a lower level in the first few months and then slowly increase it incrementally each month. The first few months may turn out to give a negative cash flow because of start-up expenses. However, you should aim to be in a positive cash flow by month six or even month three, depending on the type of business and whether money was invested in the company.*

For an established company that wants to introduce a sales forecast, it is easier as they already know how much business they have coming in, how much they want to increase business, where most of the business is coming from and via which channel (e.g. word of mouth, website, attending events/networking), so it's just a matter of being able to identify these aspects (through KPIs) and including this information in the relevant areas of the budget forecast. It is all about visibility and being able to trace performance and progress to be able to track how the company is doing and where you can introduce growth."

This is awesome advice from Gerlanda and perfect divine timing, since you, my reader, will soon be starting up your business and will need to create and implement a sales forecast before you start trading.

Obviously, I had no clue about any of this when I launched my business. I'm thankful that I have it securely in place now.

How Do You Position Yourself as an Expert?

One of the key things Gerlanda stressed to me when we met was the importance of a positive mental attitude. This is the part where you can let your soul purpose run wild and allow your enthusiasm, self-belief and passion shine through. Gerlanda explained that having the right mental state of mind helps you figure out how to position yourself.

Gerlanda believes there are three ways to position yourself – beginner, dessert or expert.

Beginner: People buy from beginners because they like the person and like what they do. Beginners will accept any type of work in order to get money coming in. They are really enthusiastic and will love what they are doing (in other words, they are connecting to their soul purpose).

Dessert: Dessert types of people are comfortable doing what they do and earning what they earn. In other words, they work to live. Dessert types are happy to 'stroll along' and make a stable income. This is not the ideal place to be, as no one living their dream should feel like they work to live; it should always be that they live to work. In addition, being stuck in this category will mean their business will never grow.

Expert: An expert has worked hard to get where they're at and still wants to grow. Experts get more deals, make bigger deals and get jobs coming to them. People buy from experts without the need to be sold to because experts add value to their services – and this is exactly where you need to be. The expert loves facing challenges and is enthusiastic. The goal is always to go from a beginner to an expert. Literally skip dessert!

Gerlanda, how quickly can it take for a person to move from being a beginner to an expert?

Gerlanda: "*By implementing strategies that give you an insight into how well your business is doing and identifying which part of your business needs improving, it is possible to be in control of your business in as little as 60 days. If you consider that, on average, there are 40 hours in a working week and 4 weeks in a month, making 160 hours worked monthly, in 60 days (2 months approximately) you could have worked 320 hours. This is achieved by treating your business as a full-time job and committing to putting the work in. Just by making small changes in your business using the tools I previously described to you and having a more in-depth insight into how your business is running, you will be able to identify what needs tweaking in order to fine tune those parts that need it so they work more effectively and to your advantage. At the end of the day, would you build a house without a plan?*"

Show What You Can Do

It is extremely important to be seen as an expert, as this is what helps you to position yourself as the leader of your niche and will, simultaneously, allow your soul purpose to shine through. Your clientele will see how much value you have, and they will want to buy your products/hire your services.

Gerlanda explains that the most effective ways in which you can position yourself as an expert is to do some or all of the following: (a) write a book, (b) write a blog, (c) create a podcast show, (d) give a presentation on the services you offer to your prospective clients, (e) deliver workshops at relevant trade and industry events, and (f) find news to share or celebrate your successes on social media platforms, the radio and in the media so you can demonstrate you are an expert at what you do.

I have done all the above and they all work in different ways. I have for sale on The Film Festival Doctor's shop page an audiobook and several e-books. These products are good marketing tools, as people see them and it encourages them to connect with me to learn more about my services.

The same applies for the blog and my podcast – they're both useful marketing tools. I make a lot of new leads when I give presentations and masterclasses at online and live industry events. Social media works brilliantly well to raise awareness of my expertise and my brand – I always post pictures that show me working for my clients and/or getting results for them, and I find that people do reach out and contact me through these platforms. Some or all the above might work for your business.

It's important that you include yourself in your social media posts to show *how* you get results for your clients. Since 2019, podcasts have become more popular than blogs and this might be more suited to your business. Research which platform your clientele likes to engage with the most and then take advantage of that medium to show how you are both an expert and a leader. I wouldn't advise you to rely on one channel exclusively; being present on one channel will simultaneously reinforce the other.

Overall, it's all about having a presence and getting into your client's mindset.

...

In the next chapter I reveal Gerlanda's effective sales pitch strategy and how to implement this essential technique in the same way as I did, so you can begin to successfully sell your services and products.

Exercises to Help You Become the Leader of Your Niche...

1. Start to create your master pipeline template – what would your pipeline look like?

2. Start to create your master KPI template – what would your KPI look like, and how would you like them to perform each month?

3. Start to create your master budget forecast template – what would it look like and how would you manage your finances?

4. Start to create your master sales forecast template – what would it look like and how much money would you like to earn each month?

5. Make a list of the three key things you need to do in order to position yourself as an expert, so you can jump straight from beginner to expert status.

6. What would you feel most comfortable doing from the list below in order to be seen as an expert in, and leader of, your niche?

    - write an e-book
    - publish books
    - write a weekly or fortnightly blog on your website

- run regular workshops

7. Most importantly, which items from this list does your audience tend to engage with the most? Whichever ones they are, think about what your content would include and how you would engage your prospective clients.

NOTES

6
HOW TO CREATE AN EFFECTIVE SALES PITCH

It's hard to believe, but many business owners don't spend much time perfecting and tweaking their all-important sales pitch. Before you can do for your client what you were born to do and live your soul purpose, you need to close a business deal with them – and this involves delivering your sales pitch.

Gerlanda Milioto explains that crafting a good sales pitch is not easy, because it is no longer a 'pitch' in the sense that you throw information at your client, as a tennis player would pitch the ball to their opponent.

She explains that in order to build trust and a strong and quick client relationship, an effective sales pitch is a two-way street – a conversation where you listen to your potential client 80% of the time and speak 20% of the time by asking real and meaningful open-ended questions to acquire information. Then, once you know their challenges and pain, that's where you can let your soul purpose shine and come in full force by explaining how you can offer them a solution.

Gerlanda's golden rule is that a good sales pitch starts with a great first impression. She reminded me that sales professionals work hard to make a memorable and positive initial impact by creating laser-focused one-liners; however, it's just as important that your short, snappy delivery also echoes long after you've delivered that opening line.

When Gerlanda taught me how to craft my sales pitch I was amazed how many key things were missing from my original attempt. I was guilty of giving my potential clients loads of information at once, rather than focusing on building rapport with them and letting them do most of the talking. Gerlanda stressed that I needed to allow them to ask me questions too, as this is a sign of interest – a lead wanting to know more about you and what you can offer is the first step towards closing a business deal. Always remember to only give away the information you need to, which will allow them to ask questions and find out more.

Although I had done okay closing deals with clients it wasn't always easy, and Gerlanda's technique showed me why it had previously been a struggle. I knew deep down before I met her that my technique needed fine tuning, but I didn't know what the tools were until I met her at that boring (but extremely worthwhile!) networking event. This chapter discusses in further detail what this toolbox is and how to craft a killer sales pitch that will help you get your business off the ground, boost your sales and generate a healthy profit.

Do Your Research

It is a cold hard fact that your product or service will not sell itself. As I've already said, it's not about throwing information at the buyer anymore. It's about constructing the most effective and successful pitch, which must always be *bespoke* to the potential client.

Gerlanda explained that making the perfect pitch requires you to understand your client, therefore if you're not researching your customer, you are severely decreasing your chances of securing the deal. Before delivering your pitch to the prospective client, you should take time to do as much *intense* research on them as you can.

During your initial contact, she said you must always be sure to ask the right questions so you can tailor your message to address their specific needs and ease the deal to the next step. Solid, careful research will also keep the buyer(s) engaged. Show them you understand who they are and what they do with a lean message that highlights the features of your product that will matter to them the most. While you are researching your lead, I would advise you to be aware of *their* clients and who they work with. You may find you have already worked with someone they also work with, and that will help strengthen the connection.

I research my clients via several platforms, including their Instagram account, their website and their IMDb page. IMDb – the Internet Movie Database – is an online database of information related to films and filmmakers, including cast and production crew. It features personal biographies, plot summaries, trivia, ratings, and reviews from fans and critics. This is my favorite way to get to know my prospective client before we begin building a relationship, as this platform tells me a lot about who they are, the quality of their work and their achievements so far. It also gives me an idea of what their budget might be.

Instagram tells me a lot about a filmmaker's personality and will often show me examples of their work through pictures and videos. Their website is also extremely useful as it often includes the slate of films they have in development (or have completed) so I can get a good impression of their aims as a filmmaker and also the 'bigger picture' vision for their production company business.

Gerlanda mentioned that my sales pitch should be different each time that I delivered it; she couldn't stress this enough. If you come in with a story from only your angle, the chances are it will not resonate with your audience. The key is to always think like your clients think. What do they want to hear? What do they want to know? If something is not relevant to your client or their needs, don't tell them about it. However, do ask questions. Always get their point of view, because you may find other areas of interest. However, be cautious of what you choose to ask. Always have in mind the kind of answer you are expecting when asking a question.

Your soul purpose will never let you down during this process. It will help guide you to understand which questions are the right ones to ask. Once when I was researching a filmmaker via IMDb, I noticed he had made two short films a few years before he made his first feature film, which he wanted to speak to me about. His short films had been seen predominantly at smaller film festivals and I wondered if he wanted his feature film to be seen at bigger festivals, especially since it was a very strong first film. So I asked him. "Yes, OMG, you read my mind!" he replied. "I really do feel that I have come on in leaps and bounds as a director since I made those other films. My feature film really is my calling card and I want to aim high." I'm pleased I closed a deal with this filmmaker and I secured the film festival screenings that he desired.

Speak to the Right People

During my training with Gerlanda, she helped me realize why it was taking me a long time to close a deal. Gerlanda stressed that all the research and customer information in the world won't help you if you aren't in touch with the actual decision maker who can approve the purchase.

I always ensured that I spoke with the producer of a film, as this is usually the decision maker when it comes to spending money. However, I began to notice that producers often needed to talk to other team members, either other producers or the film's financier. I soon realized I should have requested to speak with *all* the key people involved in the film, including the financier. Moving forwards, I began to take this approach and it was a lot more effective.

Therefore, always make sure you're speaking with the budget holder and/or decision maker of the company or relevant department. Don't speak with marketing executives unless you have talked to their boss first. When I was scheduling a call with an animation company, the producers said they would need to relay the information back to their boss to see if he would be interested in my services. I suggested that we included him in the meeting, and that helped to close the deal as he asked loads of questions (more so than the producers!) and made a decision straight away!

Before you deliver your sales pitch, ensure you are talking to the person who not only truly understands the business, but is also a decision maker. If you can't figure out who this is through your own research, don't be afraid to ask your contact at the company; they don't want their time wasted either and they'll be impressed with your courage to ask.

Show Them You Know How to Do It

This is the fun part of the sales pitch conversation as this is where you demonstrate you are the leader of your niche, the person who is always one step ahead of their competitors and is perfect for the job.

It's important during the pitch that you share your answers to a problem that your potential client is struggling with. Gerlanda loves the following quote from Guy Kawasaki, who is an established author and venture capitalist:

"Enchantment is the purest form of sales. Enchantment is all about changing people's hearts, minds and actions because you provide them a vision or a way to do things better. The difference between enchantment and simple sales is that with enchantment you have the other person's best interests at heart too."

This is the point where you let your soul purpose take center stage. You'll find this is something that will come naturally; you won't need to force anything and neither will you be lost for words, as you will know exactly what to say. For example, a client asked me at a networking event: "What can you do that I can't?"

I responded very passionately and confidently by reassuring him that "We have the type of connections, relationships and contacts with festival programmers that filmmakers don't, which helps us to create a very successful festival strategy for our clients' films and gets them the results they want."

He said, "Now that's interesting. I don't know anyone and perhaps this is what is blocking me from getting into festivals. Let's talk." We did – and we helped him to get solid results on the festival circuit.

Gerlanda explained to me that it's no secret that customers respond most positively to products and solutions that solve a current problem they could be experiencing. A successful sales pitch will acknowledge that problem (via research and careful listening) and provide a solution that best fits that buyer's needs. Gerlanda explained that even if your company only offers one product or service, each pitch should speak to the exclusive challenges of the business you're pitching to. Your message should be refined around a specific product or service feature (or features) that the specific person you're pitching to will benefit most from. Remember it's always about your client; the entire sales pitch conversation should revolve around them. If it becomes too much about you, you won't be able to close the deal.

Be Prepared to be Challenged

As you're reviewing your sales message, be sure your pitch not only includes thorough research and solves a prospective client's problem, but that the pitch also addresses potential sales objections that may come up.

Gerlanda explains that the most common sales objections fall in four buckets:

- **B**udget ("We don't have the funds.")
- **A**uthority ("I'm not the decision maker.")
- **N**eed ("I don't think we need your services right now.")
- **T**ime ("We don't have the time right now to engage your services and hire new people.")

This is also known as BANT. You may not need to have a detailed response to all four but be prepared to discuss each. The key here is to offer a reply that shows value to your buyer.

A big obstacle when working within the film industry is budget. If I was given a penny for each time a filmmaker said they didn't have the budget to work with me after an engaging sales pitch and conversation, I would be a multi-millionaire! However, if they really want to work with you then they will find the funds; you simply need to present a solution to that obstacle. When the budget problem crops up, I offer the client a different way to pay, for example, two monthly instalments, or half upfront, half two months later if it's a larger fee. It's important to let your accountant manage this with them in order to ensure they pay on time. I also like to offer them the option to pay via credit card. Budget really is the most common reason for not being able to move forwards if you have done a good job in your pitch. Gerlanda stresses that it is very important to talk to them about how much money your product or service can save them to reassure them it is a worthy investment.

Gerlanda also reminded me never to feel afraid to tell them the price or ask what their budget is. This is always a tricky thing to do, especially with filmmakers, as sometimes they don't like to reveal this and often they don't know how much money they have available to spend. Gerlanda explains that if you don't know what they can afford before delivering the price or solution, you are not going to be in a position to offer them "the best solution at the most affordable price."

She suggests telling them how much time and money they can save by using your services or product. You also need to find out what would happen to their business if their problem is not resolved – how much of an impact could it have? However, don't just come straight out and tell them: break it down for them and show them how they can benefit from each aspect. Deliver the features and follow up each feature with a benefit. For example, "We will [explain how you will resolve the problem for them] which means you won't have to waste money doing [the wrong thing]."

Once you know what problems they are facing, use this as your ammunition.

Don't Just Talk – Remember to Always Listen

Gerlanda continually reminded me never to dismiss objections but rather ask questions to verify their exact concerns and then deliver the right answer or solution. For example, you might ask if the prospective client is currently working with someone offering a product/service similar to what you offer. If they do, highlight the features that differentiate your product or service (remember, by this point you'll have already done your research, so you know their competitors, but you *have to* know yours too!).

I mentioned right at the beginning of the book that my biggest competitor was the American company, Film Festival Secrets. I identified that Chris does an amazing job offering film festival strategy consultations and coaching to filmmakers. However, he doesn't offer a service where he manages the whole festival strategy, including submitting to festivals on the filmmaker's behalf, and lobbying their film to programmers, like my business does. I use this example a lot when discussing my services with prospective clients and it helps them to better understand the landscape and what The Film Festival Doctor can do for them to solve their problems.

Gerlanda continually reassured me that over time, I would improve my objection handling and responses based on the feedback I'd be receiving from prospective clients. In the meantime, the best thing to do would be to leverage customer and product research and use that knowledge in handling objections.

To ensure you are bonding positively with your potential clients, Gerlanda suggests you always check in with them during your pitch by letting them know you relate to what they're saying, sympathizing with them when sympathy is needed, and perhaps relaying a relevant anecdote. Take the time to listen to them and respond with deep, thoughtful follow-up questions that show you are already committed to solving their problem for them. In addition, you could also tell them what you did for others facing a similar problem and how they benefited from your product/services.

She explains that this really is a truly critical step towards understanding their business needs and subsequently closing the deal. If you're listening and asking the right questions, you can adjust your sales message so it sounds really appealing to the client. If your pitch goes well, and you have your ears open, it should feel less like a business presentation and more like a healthy conversation about their business needs – a bit like helping a friend solve a problem.

The 'helping a friend' mindset quickly became the way in which I began to close deals with filmmakers. Getting to know your clients on a more human level and taking a genuine interest in them positions you as an expert, which simultaneously helps them to build trust in you and reassures them that you are the right person for the job. I always like to be myself and include some laughter and jokes in the conversation as that lightens the tone and makes things feel a lot more natural, friendly and organic.

Don't Leave the Ball in Their Court!

Even though listening to your client is critical, don't be hasty to leave after your pitch or wait for the client to define the next steps as it is not their job to do this.

Every sales pitch should end with a call to action – which you must deliver. Even if the customer isn't ready to commit and sign on the dotted line just yet, be sure to keep this prospective client on the journey and move them forward with a follow-up meeting or a trial period.

Never wait for the customer to make the call to action as they won't do this. This is solely the salesperson's responsibility and failing to be proactive could result in the meeting or relationship ending before you have achieved your goals for being there. Don't waste an opportunity or your time.

In the early days of The Film Festival Doctor when I received emails from prospective clients, I used to respond to their questions/challenges/objections with competent and detailed answers. However, I wasn't including any type of call to action. For example, I didn't say: "I'd be very interested in viewing the current cut of your film; if you could send me a link, I'd love to watch it." Or: "Let's schedule a follow up call to discuss this in further detail." I lost deals because of this. Now, however, I pose a minimum of two questions to each prospective client and nine times out of ten they respond and we begin to build a relationship.

...

And finally, never be too hard on yourself – you are just about to get started on this journey and it all comes together with practice. Another golden rule my dear friend Phil (the super connector who introduced me to Marie Diamond) told me is to never take business personally or compare yourself with your competitors. It's always important to remain emotionally detached. Some people will be very well suited to work with you and others won't be.

During the time that Gerlanda and I were working together we became good friends and she is incredibly supportive of my business. She would attend networking events with me and also came to film screenings I hosted to support my brand. I always book her for regular consultancy as I find that, from time to time, I still require help tweaking and refining my budget forecasting and sales pitches in order to keep myself in alignment.

You've now been introduced to all the key business techniques and systems you need to launch your first business. Have you enjoyed completing the tasks? I'm looking forward to seeing snapshots of your pipelines and hearing how you'll be pitching your products/services to me so I can see your leadership and "I was born to do this!" qualities emerge!

The next few chapters focus on how to implement several very important daily spiritual practices into your business infrastructure. Let's start with cosmic ordering...

Exercises to Help You Become the Leader of Your Niche...

1. Start this exercise by using Gerlanda's techniques to draft your killer sales pitch.

2. Ask for feedback from others and then work on your pitch for a few hours a week so it becomes second nature to you and you can say it without having to read it like it is a script.

3. How will your clients save money when they hire you to solve their problem?

4. How will you handle objections and challenges from your potential clients?

5. How will you respond when a potential client says they do not have the budget to hire your services?

6. How will you prove to your potential client that you really are the best person to do this job for them?

7. What type of approach will you take towards building a strong and solid rapport with your potential client?

8. How would you compare your offering to that of your competitors?

NOTES

7
HOW TO INTEGRATE COSMIC ORDERING INTO YOUR BUSINESS

When I was younger, I was very interested in spiritual techniques, though I never looked into them deeply until I had my heart broken in 2013.

My boyfriend at the time and I had an off and on, up and down type of relationship. The night before I was due to move to stunning Epping in the county of Essex in the UK, he kindly said he would help me finish my packing and I agreed to cook us dinner. I was very grateful for his offer as we'd had a bit of an argument the day before and I was feeling very anxious about our situation and where the relationship was going. During the afternoon, whilst I was buying the ingredients for our meal, he texted me to say he was feeling unwell and couldn't come over. However, he promised he would call me as soon as he was feeling better.

That night I finished packing and the following morning I moved to my lovely new apartment in Epping. I called him and left a voicemail explaining it was an amazing place and I couldn't wait for him to see it. I was expecting him to respond but I didn't hear anything, so I imagined he'd give me a call the following day.

However, I didn't hear from him again until I saw him, by chance, at a film screening event I was hosting two years later! During that two-year period, I was beside myself, wondering what was going on and if he was okay. I occasionally spoke to his mom on the phone, as I got on with her really well, and she said he was fine – but not once did he call or text me.

I was aware during this time that my ex-boyfriend had a lot of personal issues that were seriously affecting his mental and physical health. However, the situation broke me. I couldn't understand what I'd done wrong or why he was acting in this way. I almost went into a downward spiral of depression – until I was introduced to the law of attraction when I met Marie Diamond, the Feng Shui expert I introduced to you in Chapter 4. In fact, the Universe saved me from what could have been a very dark period of my life. It also helped me to understand that I wasn't to blame for what had happened with my ex. I had done nothing wrong.

I'm pleased to say my ex-boyfriend and I are now on really good terms and he is feeling a lot better in himself. When we finally had a conversation about that two-year period of silence, he explained that he just couldn't cope with the situation and couldn't speak to me about the romantic feelings he still had for me. I accepted his apology and I'm also pleased that his business, which he has worked so hard to build, is doing really well. I've fully healed from the pain and I'm glad we are both in a better place. Oddly, if I'd not been through this then I would never have discovered the world of spirituality and I would never have been open to cosmic ordering.

What Is Cosmic Ordering?

The person who introduced me to cosmic ordering was in fact Ellen Watts, who is also the person who encouraged me to write this book! I came across Ellen's extraordinary book *Cosmic Ordering Made Easier: How to Get More of What You Want - More Often* by chance via the internet.

In 2013, Michael Knight, a spiritual therapist I was working with to help me understand the ex-boyfriend situation, mentioned that he met his partner via cosmic ordering. She had written a list of everything she wanted her new partner to be, including skin color, origin, height, likes and dislikes and career etc. She then placed a cosmic order and soon afterwards she met Michael. He ticked all the boxes on her list – he was exactly what she had asked for. I never forgot his story and I knew I wanted to look into it further.

However, it wasn't until a few years later that I Googled 'cosmic ordering' and Ellen's book appeared. I ordered it straight away and it quickly became my bible, a 'go to' book that I frequently refer back to. It clearly explains what cosmic ordering is and the golden rules behind it. Ellen explains that essentially, cosmic ordering is asking the Universe for what you want – and it arrives. It's not something she has created all by herself either; rather, it's been around forever. You'll even find cosmic ordering in the Bible, where it is referred to as 'miracles.'

Ellen shares her cosmic ordering technique, which is to say: "What I really want is X" and finish by saying "For the good of all concerned." Ellen stresses that it is very important to finish each cosmic order with that final sentence as it ensures that no one should ever lose out in order for you to gain. This is very important to her when she places her orders, especially orders relating to money, as she doesn't want anyone to die in order to leave money to her.

Michael Knight told me the best way to start working with the cosmic ordering technique is to do the 'car parking order'. This is where you ask the Universe to ensure you have a parking space upon arrival in a car park. I gave it a go and it worked! I was driving to Epping one day to see a friend for coffee. It's very difficult to find a parking space in Epping, especially in the high street. I put that limiting belief aside and placed the order that what I really wanted was a parking space upon my arrival in Epping High Street, for the good of all concerned. I was driving along the high street and it was, as always, busy. All of a sudden, I noticed a car start to reverse out, leaving a parking space ready for me to park in – a miracle! Ever since then I always place this type of order when I'm driving somewhere and need to park and I always get a space – even in central London, where people believe there is nowhere to park!

It is important to remember that you must never wish for anything bad on someone else as that is just a way to create bad karma for yourself. In fact, orders asking for something bad to happen to someone else will never be delivered. Cosmic orders are about you – specifically what you want for yourself – and are therefore delivered to you. It's similar to when you go to a restaurant and place an order for your food. You order what you want to eat for yourself (pizza with a side order of chips) – not anyone else.

Another thing Ellen emphasizes is that it is important to break your cosmic order down into bitesize chunks – try to avoid asking for the 'happily ever after' result, as she calls it. This kind of cosmic ordering could be akin to "What I really want is to get married next year." Instead, break that order down into bitesize chunks – start with going out on a date, then another one, then other things that you would like to include to develop the relationship and where you want it to go next.

Shortly after reading Ellen's book I began to have consultancy sessions with her, where she helped me tweak and re-align my cosmic ordering techniques and also helped me place orders that I just didn't know how to articulate. During our sessions she encouraged me to make a note of the cosmic orders I was placing so I could keep track of them and see how well the Universe was working with me and for me. Ellen pointed out that this was a great way to figure out the blocking factors that might be standing in the way of any cosmic orders I placed that were not being delivered. Ellen calls it her 'cosmic order recorder' and it really is a useful way to keep track of your progress, as well as making notes and seeing how quickly your orders get delivered. As Ellen explains in her book, it's not an easy thing to do as you have to learn the ins and outs of the technique. However, once you get the hang of it you can easily identify what is working for you, what isn't working for you and what needs tweaking when you place your cosmic orders.

Finally, what is crucially important is to remember to always let go and do something else once you have placed your order. If you can't let go and your body and emotions feel anxious, you will block your order from coming through. Remove all emotional attachment and expectation – forget about it and trust that it's all in order (literally!) and working in your favor. For example, when I was living in Loughton, UK, I was concerned that my rent might increase after the first year. One month before my rental renewal letter was due to arrive from the estate agents, I placed the following order: "What I really want is for the rental fee on the house I currently live in, based in Loughton, Essex, to remain the same price that I am currently paying, for the good of all concerned." Exactly one month later I received the renewal letter from the estate agents saying my landlady would not be increasing the rental fee. I had completely forgotten about this order and it was delivered to me in exactly the way I had asked! It remained that same price for another year too.

The Luis Cosmic Order

I think the most memorable (and miraculous!) cosmic order I placed related to one of my favorite people, Luis – or my 'Mexican Dream', as I've nicknamed him. Ellen had mentioned that it was okay to place a cosmic order involving another person if this individual was someone I knew and was part of my inner circle.

I met Luis on the film festival circuit in Arizona 2018. Luis had starred in a film I was representing called *Frontera* and he was attending the festival to support the screening of the film with the other members of the team: the director Jake, and his best friend and co-star Omar. Luis is one of the most hilarious, sweetest people I've ever met. He has a lovely smile and is always very positive. We quickly formed a close bond and we would always hang out with each other when I was in the USA. In addition to being a great actor, Luis is also a very successful Florida-based realtor.

Before I moved to Los Angeles I was flying back and forth to the USA a lot, attending festivals and growing my business. During 2019 I stayed in an apartment in LA for two months and I was due to meet Luis when I was next in Florida attending a film festival to represent a wonderful film, *The Cunning Man*, on behalf of my client. However, I was also going to be in the USA for my birthday in August, and I really wanted to celebrate it with Luis.

I decided to place a cosmic order. "What I really want is to celebrate my birthday with Luis during the month of August, for the good of all concerned." I didn't want to specify LA or Florida, as I was open to celebrating it anywhere. When I placed this order, I had my doubts about it. I wasn't sure how this would be delivered or if I was asking for far too much. What I was experiencing was a bit of disbelief; however, this was a good thing as it helped me to remove attachment to any outcome and forget about it quicker.

I flew to Florida for the film festival and met Luis. I'd totally forgotten about the order I'd placed, but I was planning on asking him at some point during the night if he would be up for coming to Los Angeles to celebrate my birthday with me.

Shortly after he arrived, he asked me how long I was staying in LA. "Two months," I replied.

"Oh cool!" he said. "I'll be coming to LA with my brother towards the end of August to visit my aunt."

"Oh wow. When?" I asked.

"23rd to 26th," he replied.

My birthday was on the 25th August! We did indeed see each other during the time he was in LA and it was so much fun to celebrate with him – and it's all thanks to the Universe for organizing this for us!

The moral of the story is to trust that your cosmic order will be delivered – but not always in the way you expect it to come. This story also shows that miracles happen all the time (as Ellen points out in her book), and that anything is possible.

How to Fit Cosmic Ordering into Your Business Infrastructure

Every morning, shortly after waking and doing five minutes of meditation, but before I start doing my emails and getting into my exciting work routine, I place my cosmic orders and say my manifestations (which we will dive into further during the next chapter).

A lot of entrepreneurs (including rapper Jay-Z!) start each day by saying their daily goals out loud and stating their monthly goals at the start of each month. I do the same thing; however, I convert both my monthly goals and daily goals into cosmic orders.

For example, my monthly goals might be that I'd like to:

- sign up two new films to work on, which are excellent films that I can represent and help get them seen at festivals around the world
- schedule four consultations with filmmakers who need advice and support, so I can help them to achieve their film festival goals
- connect with an abundance of new business leads so I can meet more filmmakers to nurture and grow my business.

I re-word them into the following cosmic orders:

- "What I really want during the month of X is to close deals with a minimum of two new film festival management clients who have wonderful films that I can represent and who I will enjoy working with to help them get their film seen on the festival circuit, for the good of all concerned."
- "What I really want during the month of X is to schedule four consultations with filmmakers who

need advice and support, so I can help them to achieve their film festival goals, for the good of all concerned."

- "What I really want is to receive an abundance of new business leads during the month of X who can help me grow my business and introduce me to new clients who I can nurture, for the good of all concerned."

It's very important during this process not to think about money. Instead, focus on how you will feel when the orders are delivered. In my case, for example, I think positively about how amazing the film will be, which festivals I'd like to get it seen in and how much I'll enjoy nurturing these wonderful filmmakers.

The Daily Cosmic Ordering Routine

The daily cosmic orders I place are the best and most fun and after I place them, I feel extremely motivated for the day. I'm also excited by knowing they will be delivered to me without me wondering how they will arrive, what time of the day they'll come in, all those micro details. Here are the two daily cosmic orders I place each morning without fail – and I am always motived to say these. Never are they asked for in a way that is boring, mundane or as if my heart is not in it; rather, they are full of passion.

- "What I really want is for the Universe to present me with a minimum of one new business lead today who is a quality lead, a filmmaker who has a finished film and is serious about working with me and has the budget to do so, for the good of all concerned."
- "What I really want is for the Universe to present me with a minimum of one new business connection today who can lead me to grow my business and

introduce me to new clients, for the good of all concerned."

...

Sometimes you will find yourself doing an 'in the moment' cosmic order that is unplanned and spontaneous. When I was working on developing a festival strategy for a client, I just knew there were some other festivals I could add to the strategy that would be a perfect fit for his film, but I couldn't for the life of me remember what they were. My intuition nudged me to ask for help, so I asked the Universe if it could kindly present me with a list of more festivals that *Love's Labour Lost* (the name of the film) would be a perfect fit for. Two hours later they popped into my head and another one arrived via an email – which was (ironically!) informing me that the festival was open for submissions. The film was accepted into one of the festivals, where it won the Best Short Film award!

The more you get into a habit and a routine of placing your cosmic orders, the more it will become second nature to you. You won't need to keep a reminder to place your orders either; rather, you'll place the order naturally, as if you were talking and having a conversation with someone – that special someone being the Universe. Always remain calm when you place your cosmic orders and never bring anxiety into your conversations, as that shows fear. Always remain grounded and place the order when you know how to articulate what you want to ask for.

Placing your cosmic orders each morning and, when necessary, in the moment really helps you to become more positive and trusting in the process. Most importantly, it quickly becomes clearer to you that the Universe really is your best friend for life, and it will never let you down.

Manifestations are slightly different to cosmic ordering. In his book *Change Your Thoughts, Change Your Life: Living the Wisdom of the Tao*, the iconic Dr Wayne W Dyer refers to cosmic ordering as 'manifesting'. Essentially, manifesting and cosmic ordering are both ways in which you can co-create with the Universe. In the next chapter you'll learn how to differentiate and separate the two principles and integrate the second essential spiritual component into your business infrastructure.

Exercises to Help You Become the Leader of Your Niche...

1. Write down three cosmic orders you would like to place and then ask for these orders to be delivered using Ellen's cosmic ordering technique.

2. Create a 'cosmic order recorder' for yourself. Keep track of the orders, making a note of how and when they were delivered and the way in which they were delivered.

3. Keep a journal of how your perception changes when you begin to notice the ways in which your cosmic orders are being delivered to you.

4. Did all three orders arrive in the way you expected?

5. If one (or all) of your orders didn't arrive in the way you expected, can you identify what the blocking factors could have been? Use your 'cosmic order recorder' template to help you progress.

NOTES

8
HOW TO INTEGRATE MANIFESTING INTO YOUR BUSINESS

How did it feel placing your first cosmic order?! Exciting, isn't it? As discussed in Chapter 4, the law of attraction is a powerful thing and when you know how to use it, it can really help you to manifest what you want and do what you were born to do. Manifesting is, in fact, something that everyone does on a daily basis, whether consciously or unconsciously. This is another technique that will cultivate more magic in your business.

The website www.thelawofattraction.com explains that there are many different 'definitions' of the word manifest, but the simplest would be (in spiritual terms) that a manifestation is 'something that is put into your physical reality through thought, feelings, and beliefs'.

This means that whatever you focus on is what you are bringing into your reality. You can manifest through meditation, visualization or via your conscious or subconscious mind. For example, if you have been thinking about getting a new job and you focused on exactly what you wanted and when you wanted it, your thoughts and feelings would be strong surrounding this.

You could then try to meditate or visualize your goals, which can help to manifest your dream new job into your reality.

Clearly, manifestations are similar to but a little different from cosmic ordering, as you don't begin manifesting by saying "What I really want is..." and you can also manifest without words; it can all be done visually in your mind, or you can say what you want quietly in your head as opposed to out loud. However, when using the cosmic ordering and manifesting principles together it actually helps you get what you want quicker.

Each morning, after I've placed my cosmic orders, I then say my affirmations, which help me to feel the positive feelings that I have cultivated in my mind, body and soul, ready for when I receive the cosmic orders. In general, manifesting should be a part of everyone's daily life as it helps put you in alignment with what you want – your goals, dreams and the feelings your heart desires. When manifesting becomes a part of your daily routine it helps to reduce any fears that are blocking you from moving forwards and builds trust in yourself, the Universe and, of course, your business! Similar to cosmic ordering, it changes your perception and strengthens your intuition as you become a person who is more willing to believe in the process and you begin to get closer and have more faith in your best friend – the Universe.

There are literally hundreds and hundreds of books on manifesting and how to manifest using the law of attraction. This chapter will simplify the process. However, I would recommend the following books as a good starting point:

- *The Secret* by Rhonda Byrne (as mentioned in Chapter 4)
- *You Are a Badass at Making Money: Master the Mindset of Wealth* and *You Are a Badass: How to Stop Doubting*

Your Greatness and Start Living an Awesome Life, both by Jen Sincero
- *I'm Worth More: Realize Your Value. Unleash Your Potential* by Rob Moore
- *You Can Heal Your Life* by Louise L Hay

A New Way to Manifest

Before I met my intuitive business consultant, Nand Harjani, I was manifesting in the way all the books and spiritual magazines told me to manifest. Back in 2013 when I was trying to understand the ex-boyfriend situation, I used to subscribe to three spiritual magazines published in the UK: *Spirit & Destiny*, *Natural Health* and *Soul & Spirit*. By no means were they trashy magazines; they were actually quite interesting and good starting points to move forwards on my spiritual journey. They provided me with the stepping stones to get me into the mindset of affirming what I wanted.

These magazines always included lots of suggestions on how to create your own manifestations and how to get into a routine and repeat them to yourself on a daily basis. The manifestations covered all aspects of daily life, including wellbeing, wisdom, romantic relationships, money and career.

Some people refer to affirmations as manifestations. They are connected, as affirmations are positive statements in the present tense that relate to what it is you want to manifest.

The type of manifestations I used to say were "I am strong," "I am a successful businesswoman who runs a thriving business," "I am confident," "I am in the best physical, mental and emotional health," "I am enough," and "I believe and trust the Universe." These manifestations were effective to a point – they did help me get into a better mindset and I did feel a little stronger and more focused on my business. At the time I had poor digestion because of the stress of the situation and affirming that I was in good health all over my body helped me to attract a very helpful nutritionist who gave me lots of useful advice and supplements to take in order to help ease that problem.

I always knew in the back of my mind that something was missing. My manifestations needed some kind of work, or perhaps I needed to use a different technique. However, I followed the blueprint and exemplary templates from the books and those three magazines, which I'd read from cover to cover, and I kept affirming what I wanted to cultivate.

It wasn't until a dear friend called Ava recommended I visit an intuitive consultant, Nand Harjani, that my way of manifesting changed dramatically...

Nand's Technique

Nand is the founder of Creative Life Sciences, based in Long Beach, California. He has developed many training programs that teach his students how to understand and work with the body's electromagnetic field. He is also widely known for his highly accurate and effective personal and business-related intuitive readings, healings, and public talks. I work with Nand frequently; his spiritual guidance is always spot on, and I can't recommend him highly enough. If you want accurate and insightful clarity on any aspect of your life, you really should see him.

When I recited my manifestations to Nand, he said they were lacking in specificity, clarity, and focus. He told me that was the reason why the outcomes were very general, confusing and not as successful as I wanted them to be. He told me I needed to introduce more detail and change the wording as that would change the energy behind my intentions. The main problem was there was a lack of focus and exactness in my affirmations. He explained that if the affirmation is not clear and exact, the outcome is vague and general. As an example, if the affirmation asks for rain, then somewhere, sometime there will be rain. This is what Nand calls an example of a general affirmation. However, modifying the affirmation by making it more specific, such as: "It will rain at the intersection of High Street and Church Road, London, United Kingdom at 4 pm on the (current) Queen of England's birthday this year," gives a clear and precise affirmation that's much more effective.

By adding more detail into my affirmations, Nand helped me to dramatically change the content of each one so they became a lot more specific, focused and clear. Amazingly, when I began to say an affirmation that was this specific and detailed, it became much easier for me to visualize what I wanted when I was saying it and also to feel the emotions and positive energy surrounding what I wanted.

My short and sweet "I believe and trust the Universe" affirmation changed to "It is my intent to have no fear and self-doubt within me and to completely trust the direction the Universe is guiding me through for the sake of continuously enchanting and growing my relationships, my business and myself."

Have a go yourself at saying this affirmation. You will notice that your perception, mindset and outlook will change. When I said this every morning, I always emphasized the word 'trust' – showing the Universe that I meant what I was saying, that I did trust it implicitly and that it was the guiding force helping me to grow my relationships. It really worked, as soon after I was having healthier romantic relationships, my business was thriving and I felt different in myself – more confident for sure as a businesswoman, and more grounded and less fearful about the challenges that one faces when running a business. I felt I had reached a point where I wouldn't let anything faze me or become dramatic. Rather, when a challenge occurred, I'd not respond with fear and instead felt the feeling(s) in my body and resolved the situation professionally and to the best of my ability, and with kindness. That, in fact, is what a leader does – and I learnt this through powerful manifesting.

Say It Like You Mean It

Nand also pointed out that what is also extremely important when saying my manifestations each morning is to literally say them like I mean them – say them in the way in which you want what you want to happen; show the Universe you are serious about this happening and you really want them to happen in reality. This is called 'feeling the feelings'.

Feeling or experiencing feelings can be quite uncomfortable and challenging as sometimes we don't want to feel unpleasant emotions. I realized that, for a very long time, instead of feeling the feeling of fear, letting it pass through my body and experiencing what it feels like so I could come out the other side stronger, I had unconsciously avoided feeling it and instead thought of positive things, which stopped it from doing what it needed to do. I let good feelings pass through me, but I couldn't allow anything that was not good to go through me as I didn't want to look weak in front of others, and I also didn't want to spiral into depression. However, when Nand told me how to do this I allowed my body to experience these feelings and it helped me remove a lot of excess baggage that I wasn't aware I was carrying.

Nand encouraged me to be aware of any sensations that I felt in my body, as this was an important part of the process too. He said that when you are aware of how your body is responding and you are in tune with it, your life will be more productive instead of being held back – and he was right. I now feel more connected with myself and my body and in tune with it than I ever was previously. I'm especially grateful that I learnt this technique prior to the COVID-19 global pandemic that occurred at the start of 2020.

The COVID-19 Affirmation

Along with everyone else in the world, I'm sure you were shaken up by the COVID-19 pandemic. No one was expecting to be told to stay at home and for the whole world to shut down. Neither was the world prepared to learn and practice social distancing.

When the COVID-19 pandemic hit it caused everyone – and especially business owners – to become full of fear and uncertain of everything. The one thing I was certain about was that I would not let the fear surrounding this pandemic affect either my business or my wellbeing. I drafted a specific affirmation with Nand that I began saying from the start of the first day of the lockdown:

"It is my intent for my business to thrive and grow each and every day during the COVID-19 pandemic. I receive an abundance of film festival screening invitations every day for my clients' films, and new business leads, and I close a lot of new business deals during this period with clients who pay promptly. All my current clients are very happy with our customer care and support and their films are doing great on the festival circuit and winning an abundance of awards."

The way in which I said this each morning was not in a rushed, monotone, 'reading off a page' voice like I wasn't connected to it. Instead, within my voice you could feel the drive, motivation and unstoppable force that came from the core of my soul purpose, from an entrepreneur who would not give in to the fear surrounding this pandemic and believe every single fearful news report that was flying around.

Every time I said it, I almost shouted the words THRIVE and GROW and I said them exactly like I meant them. I was taking this seriously and I would do whatever it took to reach my desired outcome.

From the start of the pandemic right until things started to get back to normal my business continued to thrive and carried on as it normally would. The pandemic brought a lot of good things with it; for example, several of my clients' short films that were stuck in post-production or put on the back burner were actually finished because of editors being able to work remotely from home. Filmmakers made films during the pandemic that focused on isolation, and a lot of film scripts were written and subsequently funded, ready to be made after the pandemic. Saying the COVID-19 pandemic affirmation every day, in addition to placing my cosmic orders, helped me and my business stay balanced in times of radical uncertainty and change, for which I am truly grateful.

One of the things you'll notice when you begin manifesting is your feelings will lead the way, and it is your feelings that will subtly tell you if this is what you really want. If you don't feel the passion and commitment in your voice then it won't manifest, as subconsciously your mind is telling you that you don't really want it. It will eventually become clear to your conscious mind what is important to you and what your priorities are. If what you are saying becomes mundane and routine, and you are not feeling the emotions, this is when you should review your manifestations and consider if they are really what you want, and which parts of them need tweaking. Always keep them fresh!

The Importance of a Vision Board

Another tool that can help you manifest more swiftly and comfortably is a vision board.

A vision board is a visualization tool comprising a board (of any sort) that you use to build a collage of words and pictures that represent your goals and dreams. Vision boards provide you with a daily visual reminder of these dreams and goals. The reason vision boards work so well is because you see them every day. Most importantly, the images you place on your vision board must reflect your goals and dreams and they must be images that you are drawn to and that you want to look at every day. Photos, quotes, sayings, images of places you want to go, reminders of events, places and people, postcards from friends – in other words, just about anything that will inspire you.

There are many different ways in which one can create and design a vision board; Marie Diamond has even created her own Feng Shui-style vision board that she sells on her website. The golden rule is that the Universe requires words and pictures. However, as Jack Canfield points out in his book *21 Ways to Make Your Vision Board More Powerful*, it is very important to keep it neat. He urges people to avoid creating a cluttered or chaotic vision board – as you don't want to attract chaos into your life. He also mentions that it is important to add motivational 'affirmation words' and inspiring quotes that represent how you want to FEEL, like 'courage', 'love', or 'imagination'. This I strongly agree with; however, on my vision board I give more context to those general words such as 'love' by adding examples like "I am loving living in my apartment in LA on Miracle Mile and working hard while overlooking the beach."

Marie Diamond stresses (and I strongly agree) that it is crucial to put a picture of yourself in the center of your board, as you are the one who is the center of your universe. The center of my vision board has a picture of me holding several awards that I've helped my clients win. Surrounding this photo are things that are important to me.

It is also very important to get into a routine of looking at your vision board several times a day, ideally first thing in the morning and before you go to bed. Looking at pictures related to what you want helps you to feel the feelings you want to cultivate more easily. I highly recommend you look at your vision board just before you say your manifestations and place your cosmic orders, as the images are fresh in your mind, you are in alignment with what you want and it inspires you to become more creative in the way you deliver your manifestations.

My vision board is in my office. I can literally see it from the corner of my left eye so it's always there when I look up and it reminds me what to focus on. I have a picture of Oprah Winfrey on it looking strong; beside the image is a quote from her: "The reason I've been able to be so financially successful is because my focus has never ever for one minute been money." That is an example of an inspirational quote that's spot on and truthful. When I look at that, it helps me put my whole business into perspective.

I'd highly recommend you create a vision board that includes everything you want to manifest. The images can be photos, cut outs from magazines or images from the internet – whatever inspires you. The images you choose to place on your vision board need to represent or symbolize the experiences, feelings and possessions you want to attract into your life. The key areas to include are health, wealth, wellbeing, business, relationships, success and wisdom. You don't have to include all those aspects, only the ones that are an absolute priority to you.

You can also create a vision board that is specific to just one thing – for example, I created a vision board for my move to LA, which included images and words relating to the vision for my business in the USA, my book, my online coaching courses and my personal lifestyle. A vision board specific to just one thing, or one area of your life, helps you to live your life in the way you have created it in your mind, and to feel your future.

I always create a new vision board at the start of each year. I collect all my images during December and tend to review which pictures are important to me over the Christmas period. The start of a new year is the best time to create a new vision board as your goals and priorities change, therefore it's important to show the Universe your goals and the images that resonate with you each year on your vision board.

The main reason why I placed my vision board in my office is because that is the room where I spend 90% of my time! Wherever you spend the most time, place your vision board where you can see it and where you will be able to look at it as often as possible every day.

As a tool, the vision board is extremely effective. Jack Canfield explains that it can really help you feel the future you have designed for yourself and it also helps you to feel very grateful for the good that is currently in your life.

Cosmic ordering and manifesting are both very powerful tools when fused together, but when you implement both these techniques in your business it's extremely important to get the balance right. I focus cosmic ordering on one area and manifestation on another important area. This helps me become at peace and in alignment and harmony with my clients' energy. It also helps us work together more closely as a team and become 'one'.

So, now you know how to incorporate the techniques of cosmic ordering and manifestation in your daily routine before you get to work (and start doing things like monitoring your pipeline and KPIs etc., as outlined by Gerlanda in Chapters 5 and 6), the next questions I am always asked are: what does it really feel like to do what you are born to do? And what happens when all of what I have described so far comes together? That's the focus of the next chapter and it's a riot – come and join me for the ride!

Exercises to Help You Become the Leader of Your Niche…

1. Draft three manifestations that are important to you. Use Nand's technique and add as much specific detail as possible so each one is in alignment with your intentions.

2. Rehearse them – say them out loud. How does this feel? What feelings do you experience in your body?

3. Does your energy change? If so, how? Do you feel calmer, focused, more inspired etc.?

4. Keep saying these affirmations each day and make a note of the feelings and sensations your body experiences. Share your experiences via Instagram and don't forget to tag me.

NOTES

9
TYING IT ALL TOGETHER! HOW TO LOVE DOING WHAT YOU WERE BORN TO DO

It might be hard to believe what I'm about to say after all that you have read in this book so far, but I was not a spiritual, grateful or positive person until the age of 29. It was only then that I really started to love doing what I was born to do. As discussed in Chapter 7, it was a difficult relationship that took me down the spiritual path and has now helped me to share with you the tools that turned my life around, grow a thriving business and become a leader.

I had horrendous anxiety when I was younger. I couldn't drive or be a passenger in a car on any journey longer than 30 minutes, as I was worried I would have a panic attack during a traffic jam and there would be nowhere to stop the car and get some fresh air. I feared that if I wasn't able to get out of the car, I would die. I look back on that dark period and can't believe that my brain thought such irrational thoughts or that I used to engage with those thoughts. This was all triggered by what I call the 'Kill Bill' story.

The Kill Bill Story

Watching Quentin Tarantino's film *Kill Bill* in 2003 at Cheltenham Odeon was an experience I will never forget, and not because of how great the film was, but because of what happened during the screening. The evening screenings were all sold out, so we decided to sneak out of university lectures that afternoon and see it before anyone else. As it was the first screening of the film during the daytime, the cinema was almost empty; there were only 10 people there.

Forty minutes into the film and my friends and I were loving it. However, all of a sudden someone sitting at the front of the cinema had a violent epileptic fit and had to leave the cinema immediately to seek assistance. It was quite traumatizing to see. Later that day, I was driving to a restaurant for dinner with some friends when I got stuck in traffic. There was a massive long queue because of an accident. Out of nowhere, and without any warning whatsoever, I had a severe panic attack and needed to pull over and calm myself down. However, there was nowhere to pull over on that particular stretch of road, so I was trapped. That 15 minutes of stopping and starting in the traffic jam felt like an eternity and from that day onwards for three years I had frequent panic attacks and crippling anxiety.

The panic attacks weren't the result of seeing the person have an epileptic fit during the *Kill Bill* screening; rather, this was something that triggered a deep-rooted childhood issue that I needed to address. I didn't know what it was at the time, but I went on a downward spiral. I stopped eating proper meals and started instead to snack, to the point where I became borderline anorexic. I was diagnosed with a huge number of food allergies that I still have to this day, though thankfully have under control now. My periods stopped completely and my hair began to fall out after I washed it because of so much stress. And then came more panic attacks when I was in traffic – I couldn't stop thinking about being trapped in the car forever and unable to get out alive.

I experienced very irrational thinking, which made me a difficult person to be around. Thankfully, I found help through a therapist via the university I was studying at and she taught me about CBT (Cognitive Behavioral Therapy) and gave me a toolbox of techniques to help get rid of those feelings. Looking back on it now, I realized I was scared to feel the feelings I was experiencing. Instead, I was avoiding them and believing the stories I kept telling myself in my head were true, which made me become more fearful about everything and of course have another panic attack.

A few years later I was diagnosed with GAD – General Anxiety Disorder. I will always have that anxiety gremlin inside me but now I'm better equipped and more knowledgeable about the issue, and more trusting in the Universe to help me through life, it's nowhere near as bad as it was back in 2003. Now when I feel anxious, I let the feelings pass through me instead of avoiding them.

I never wanted to experience the type of panic attacks that I did back then, and I wouldn't want you to either. However, there was a time during 2015 when they almost came back. I was having a hard time with a client as he didn't believe we were doing the work that we had done for his film, as he was expecting results overnight. Despite showing him the timeline and how the process worked he wouldn't believe anything I was telling him, and this was extremely stressful. During a meeting with his lawyer, I showed him the evidence and all the emails I had sent to our film festival contacts pitching his film and officially submitting it to film festivals. Thankfully, a few days before the meeting the first (of many) film festival screening invitations came in, proving that we were working for him and he had got his first result. Several months later he apologized to me, we made our peace and I made a vow never to work with him again. What this experience flagged up to me – and the reason why the anxiety-driven panic attacks almost crept back into my life – was that I never wanted my clients to feel unhappy with my service, as I love working for them and there is no reason for them to be dissatisfied. Our intentions are always for the best, and it's never a case of just working with them for the money, it's always for love.

How to Prepare Yourself Before You Start Working with a New Client

In order to reduce my anxiety around client satisfaction, I always place a specific cosmic order at the start of each new project. Just after the client and I have signed the contract and before Shelagh and I begin to create the client's film festival strategy, I place a cosmic order asking (a) that the client gets more value than they pay for, (b) they receive an abundance of film festival screening invitations for their film, (c) they win awards and (d) they are ultimately satisfied with our service.

As soon as I place these orders, I always notice that I am more perceptive and open to finding ways to go the extra mile for that client and give them a thorough and bespoke service. A great example of this was a South African film my company represented called *Kings of Mulberry Street*. The Film Festival Doctor is known across South Africa as the 'South African Film Doctor', as we represent a lot of films from this territory. Aside from the fact there are no other film festival consultants like me within the South African film industry, I have strong strategic partnerships with all the key funding bodies and sales agents there who direct and recommend filmmakers to me. This is all thanks to Pascal Schmitz, who runs one of the largest sales companies, AAA Entertainment. Pascal recommends me to everyone, and we love working with him and are grateful to have him as a strong part of our network.

I adored working on this film. We achieved the client's goals by presenting the film to festival programming teams we knew from experience would like the film and would be open to screening it.

This was essentially a children's film; however, it was very innovative, had an original story and was executed brilliantly by its director, Judy Naidoo. It was not just a film for kids either; people of all ages could relate to it and enjoy it. It had the potential to travel the world as it was not limited to screenings in only South Africa, and neither was it a 'local' film that only South African people could engage with. It had worldwide star quality and I was determined to help it become a festival favorite.

Before I begin working with a client, we always discuss their goals. After a successful local theatrical release in its home country, the creative team of *Kings of Mulberry Street* were simply looking to get the film screened outside of Africa and as far and wide at as many high-end film festivals as possible. I knew we could achieve this and more for them.

The film screened in competition at 15 festivals, including the St. Louis International Film Festival, the Mill Valley International Film Festival and the Pan African Film Festival, all based in the USA and all Academy Award Qualifying events. It also screened at several children's and young people's film festivals that are part of the well-known European Children's Film Association, including BUFF Malmo in Sweden, and Cinekid in The Netherlands, and it won the Seattle Kids Film Festival's Best Feature Film Award. This was an amazing result and the emails saying we had been selected put a huge smile on my face. Those were exciting, happy times and I felt a huge sense of achievement.

Before I start working on a client's film, I know intuitively that I need to be in the best of health. I also remember to always put myself first and manifest that I am in the best physical, mental and emotional health and can face the daily challenges that all business owners have. I have an image on my vision board of a big bouquet of flowers with the words "I am in the best physical, mental and emotional health and for that I am truly grateful" underneath it, which I always remember to look at each day.

Being the Film Festival Doctor

As you know by now, I LOVE my job and it is a part of my identity, since this is what I was born to do. The best part of my business is getting results for our clients – specifically, securing film festival screening invitations for their films and nurturing our clients on their journeys around the festival circuit.

Another exciting part of this process is attending film festivals with our clients. Networking, seeing their films on screen, and helping them win awards is an amazing experience. At the time of writing this book, my company has helped our clients win over 800 awards since we began trading in 2010.

This is down to several key components, including positioning myself as an expert in order to attract and work with trailblazing visionary filmmakers who have made films that festivals will love, and using manifestation and cosmic ordering to get the best results possible for those films.

Luis' film *Frontera* was my 'little film that could'; I achieved much more for it than I expected and received more than I asked for. *Frontera* took a long time to complete; it was a passion project for its director Jake and the co-producer, co-writer and lead actor Omar. It's not unusual for an independent film to take a long time to complete as many of the people who work on it may be doing things for free or for a reduced fee and this can slow down the process somewhat. *Frontera* began shooting in LA during 2015 and was finally completed in 2018, which was when Jake and Omar were ready to take it to the circuit.

Jake discovered me and my brand through the way in which I positioned myself as an expert at a film industry masterclass I was invited to give by an LA-based company called The Industry Workshops on how to create a successful film festival strategy. Jake wasn't able to attend the event himself; however, he asked the organizer for my details as he had a problem: he was new to the festival scene and didn't know how to start submitting his film, or which festivals were the right ones to enter. During our initial meeting Jake engaged with my sales pitch and my Big Domino Statement and we closed a deal shortly after we spoke with Omar.

The contract was duly signed, and I was quickly placing my cosmic orders and visualizing a successful festival run for the film. Jake and Omar had two clear and simple goals: to get the film seen at festivals, and to find a distribution deal. Omar was also keen to find more acting opportunities as that was his passion, and Jake wanted to get more directing work. *Frontera* was, in all honesty, a hard sell to festivals. Although it was very well-acted and crafted, there wasn't anything original or ground-breaking about its story. Jake had his heart set on the Austin Film Festival, but I pointed out to him that it was not suitable for *Frontera* and that we should aim for a different level and tier of festival. There was, however, a home for it at festivals based within America, because it had the type of story that would resonate with American audiences.

I kept the festival campaign focused on predominantly only this particular territory and submitted it to 11 film festivals whose programmers would like this type of film and would see the potential and value in it. It screened at six film festivals within the USA, where it was well received. It also won a whopping eight awards, which was way more than I asked the Universe for when I placed the cosmic orders and manifested my desired outcome for the film. Winning that cluster of awards really was the icing on the cake.

The film premiered at a film festival in Laughlin, Nevada and during the awards ceremony we won a hat trick of awards. Hearing the film's name called out so many times was incredible; my heart started pumping and adrenaline rushed through me throughout the awards ceremony. I was on a high all night and the feelings of contentment and elation remained in my heart for the next couple of days whilst the festival was still in full swing. I was happy for my clients and that Omar and Jake's hard work had paid off; they didn't give up and it was all worth it for them. I loved celebrating the film's success with them as it really felt like we were a connected team and experiencing so much happiness together.

Towards the end of its festival run I also helped secure a worldwide distribution deal for the film, as well as talent management representation for Omar and Luis. This was all thanks to my soul purpose guiding me in the right direction so I could create the right strategy for the film, which got *Frontera* into the right festivals and put it in front of the right people at the right time. Just like my Gerlanda Milioto story, you never know who you are going to meet.

The Importance of Gratitude

I can't believe that, when I was younger, worrying about having another panic attack and whether I could get through a 30-

minute car journey, I never knew how to be grateful – or what gratitude really was. I am, and always will be, eternally grateful to the Universe for protecting me during that time. I became a much happier and more positive person when I began feeling and expressing my gratitude each day. A lot of things changed, both for myself and my business, when I did this. Gratitude really helps contribute towards loving what you do.

Gratitude means thankfulness and is essentially a feeling of appreciation towards the giver of kindness, gifts, help, favors, and all other types of generosity. Marie Diamond was the first member of my tribe to introduce me to the concept of gratitude. The first affirmation related to gratitude that she taught me was "I am eternally grateful that I am in the best physical, mental and emotional health and that I can share my gifts with the whole wide world." As soon as I said it, I felt a slight shift in me – I felt calmer, but I could also imagine being in the best of health, traveling around the world living my best life with my clients, with the Universe alongside me, always supporting and protecting me, no matter what.

It is extremely important to always be grateful and to say thank you for everything. If you start to become too self-centered, take people and things for granted and aren't thankful for what you have, you'll never get more of what you desire, and your energy will become toxic. When you begin to express gratitude on a daily basis and thank the Universe when your cosmic orders come in and your manifestations become reality, you'll notice that it will never stop, and you'll experience an endless flow of abundance. The moment *Frontera* won its first award at the Laughlin Film Festival I whispered, "Thank you!" to the Universe – and look what happened, another two awards came along half an hour later!

I tend to look at my vision board in the morning and I glance at it throughout the day whilst I'm working in my office. I totally agree that one should look at their vison board before they go to bed; however, my main priority before I go to sleep is to thank the Universe by expressing my gratitude. This technique can be performed either by talking out loud to yourself or, if you find it easier to give thanks through writing in a journal or a gratitude diary, that can work too.

My therapist Jessica encouraged me to write down three things I'm grateful for at the end of each day. If you do this exercise you will always find many more than three things to be grateful for, because lots of amazing and miraculous things happen each day. You'll notice this when you become more perceptive and begin to co-create with the Universe. When I lie in bed before I go to sleep, the first thing I do is say thank you to the Universe for a wonderful day, no matter what challenges occurred. Then I single out three things that happened during the day that were super exciting and filled me with joy and happiness. It's also useful to say thank you to the Universe for protecting you from something unpleasant that might have occurred, and to be grateful for the support and wisdom that the Universe provided you with.

It will get to the point where you love being grateful and expressing your gratitude every day. You'll also begin to feel extremely content, safe and trusting of the process that you're going through, both inside and outside of your body.

Get Inspired!

One thing I have to keep reminding myself of – and this will definitely apply to you too – is to not become emotionally attached either to my clients or the results I want to secure for them. The way to do that, besides continually trusting in the process and never losing faith in the Universe, is to make sure you have other activities in your life that you love.

When I worked as a personal assistant, I used to believe I had not had a productive day unless I had worked continuously for the eight hours I was sitting in an office. I soon realized you are actually not productive if you force yourself to work that much. Nowadays I tend to wake up early, meditate, manifest and do some hard-core grafting between 6 am and 11 am. Then I do other things. I like to get my priority jobs done first and for the rest of the day I'm 'on call', so to speak, and available to get back to people on emails, attend to new things that come in, have meetings and scheduled consultations with clients, do group coaching, resolve any problems that might come up and be there to support my team and my clients.

However, while I'm 'on call' I also do other things that are not business-related, including:

Cooking – I'm not the world's best cook; however, my nutritionist gave me lots of vegan recipes and I enjoy trying them and find them extremely relaxing to make, especially her homemade guacamole.

Cleaning – I know this is a bit sad, but tidying the house, even sorting out a drawer or a cupboard can be very therapeutic. In addition, it gets your home in order and is a very rewarding job when you set it out as a task to complete.

Lingerie and dresses – If you visit my website www.rebekahlouisasmith.com you'll notice I am a huge fan of clothes. I love beautiful lace lingerie to the point where I collect it! I love wearing a new dress and lingerie set for the first time when I attend a film festival. I also love collaborating with local and boutique clothing designers, whom I connect with via Instagram. When I wear their clothing at film festivals, it makes the whole experience even more fun because I feel and look great. I spend lots of time in the evenings looking at clothing companies on Instagram – it's the best platform for it, as it's all visual imagery. As I mentioned in Chapter 4, my favorite clothing brands are Bluebella, Bella Sorella and Silk Fred.

Walking – no matter what I'm doing or how busy I am, I always make time for an hour-long walk – it helps you feel fit, strong and healthy. Walking is the gentlest form of exercise and is an amazing stress relief technique, as getting outside in the open air is very relaxing, especially when you are surrounded by nature.

...

That's it – you're almost there! I bet you must feel super excited about your business and what's on the horizon for you. By now you have probably reached the stage where you can't wait to launch your business. Below you will find the last set of important tasks to complete. The final chapter of this book will remind you what to do next and how to stay in continual alignment with your soul purpose.

Exercises to Help You Become the Leader of Your Niche...

1. Visualize and feel the feelings you want to experience when you get results for your clients (in other words, when you have resolved their pain).

2. Make a note of the feelings you want to cultivate. Keep the note in a safe place and return to it once you've got the business up and running.

3. Create an action plan (a sketch book is fine) outlining how you will integrate your manifestations and cosmic orders into both your business model and your personal life – what areas are most important to you?

4. How will you detach and distract yourself from any specific outcome?

5. What hobbies and interests will you be interested in learning or taking up to distract yourself?

6. How will you express your gratitude each day? For example, will you keep a diary or give thanks out loud before you finish for the day? There's no right or wrong way – the most important thing is to get into a routine.

NOTES

CONCLUSION
NOW GO AND SHINE YOUR LIGHT AROUND THE WORLD!

Well done for coming this far. Congratulations! You made it – well done! Let's go back to the questions I asked at the beginning of the book:

1. Are you willing to do whatever it takes?
2. Will you show up every day and put the work in?
3. Are you obsessed with your business (or your business idea)?
4. Are you committed to discovering what your soul purpose is?
5. Are you able to adjust your business model where necessary?
6. Are you committed to your business for life?
7. Are you willing to learn more about yourself through your business?
8. Are you willing to integrate spiritual techniques into your business?
9. Are you committed to being the face and leader of your brand?
10. Are you a quitter?

Did you still answer yes to questions 1-9 and no to question 10?

Good! This means you are certainly NOT a quitter and you are well ahead on your journey to make your business dreams come true. Also, your passion and energy towards your business should now be at 110% as you will no doubt feel very different within yourself since you began reading this book.

Take a look at your notebook, as I imagine it will contain tons of valuable insights about what you are born to do and the direction and shape your business is beginning to take. By all means, re-visit the tasks at the end of each chapter, as you may find that more ideas and inspiration occur as your journey progresses and you receive further information.

Always remember to keep writing in your notebook and take it everywhere with you – keep it in your handbag or briefcase – as you'll continue to feel inspired and more ideas will flow to you now you have tuned into your soul purpose.

One final thing to add to your notebook is what I call The Four Ds – or, if you prefer, you can of course print them out and stick them on your fridge so you can look at them each day, first thing in the morning. The Four Ds help you stay in alignment with your soul purpose and help you to run your business successfully. They're great to meditate upon each morning and they also come in useful if you find yourself having difficulty resolving a problem for a client. The Four Ds remind you that you will always find a solution.

The Four Ds are:

Drive: Your soul purpose will always drive you to grow and nurture your business and continue to resolve your clients' problems with ease.

Discipline: Your soul purpose will give you the discipline to competently run your business and never give up.

Determination: Your soul purpose will give you the determination to work hard to get the results your clients want and for your business to succeed.

Delivery: Your soul purpose will help you deliver results for yourself and your clients and go as far and wide as possible to resolve their problems.

The Four Ds will always remind you that all the energy you are putting in is worth it. They'll also keep you firmly on track and in alignment with your 'why'.

....

As discussed in the Introduction, the journey doesn't stop when you've finished reading the book! Follow me on Instagram @borntodoitbook and share your stories with me, as I'd really love to hear from you. Tag me and I promise I will engage with your stories personally; I will also proudly share them with my tribe of followers so everyone can see your progress and growth.

Plus, as previously discussed, I can also work with you on a one to one basis, helping you to tune into your soul purpose so you can do what you were born to do. Visit my website for further information www.rebekahlouisasmith.com or drop me an email at rebekah@rebekahlouisasmith.com.

And of course, for those of you who need help getting your film accepted into film festivals, you know which doctor to call: The Film Festival Doctor! www.thefilmfestivaldoctor.com.

Thank you for sharing your journey with me and I can't wait to hear all about what's coming up next for you.

ACKNOWLEDGEMENTS

My heartfelt thanks and gratitude to all those people who have helped me write and publish this book and become who I am today: one of the leaders of my business niche.

To my mother and father, Sheila and Tony Smith, for being wonderful parents, always supporting what I do and believing in my mad ideas!

To my incredible clients, from all over the world, who were a source of inspiration while I was writing this book.

To my business team, who have provided me with an abundance of inspiration, advice, knowledge and support.

To my closest friends, who always inspire me and make me laugh.

To my coaches and mentors, who continually help to guide and support me on my business and personal journeys.

To Ellen Watts and her company, Butterfly House Publishing; without her support and encouragement to write this book it would still be only an idea in my mind!

And lastly, a big thanks to you, my reader; welcome to my inner circle.

ABOUT THE AUTHOR

Dr Rebekah Louisa Smith (aka Rebekah Film Dr) was born in Worcestershire, United Kingdom. From humble beginnings working as a personal assistant at several corporate companies, she worked her way to become an award-winning consultant and media personality who now has over 10 years of film festival strategy consulting experience.

After choosing not to pursue a career in academia, Rebekah began her film industry career in 2009, working as one of the producers of Wales' most successful national horror film festival, the Abertoir Horror Festival, which is part of the prestigious European Fantastic Film Festivals Federation.

Rebekah and the hard-working team behind her company, The Film Festival Doctor, are creators of success and are committed to nurturing filmmakers in order to help them secure film festival screenings and win awards and positive recognition within the film industry. Currently her company has won over 800 awards for their clients and her team has supported over 848 creatives across the world, enlightening and inspiring their journey towards achieving their goals and following their filmmaking dreams.

Described by many of her clients as a deeply knowledgeable and inspirational mentor, Rebekah supports individuals to adopt new strategies, mindsets and communication techniques that produce extraordinary results.

Instagram: @borntodoitbook

Email: rebekah@rebekahlouisasmith.com

INTERVIEW WITH DR REBEKAH LOUISA SMITH

Interview by Hannah Martin, Founder of The Talented Ladies Club

Ever dreamed of becoming an Oscar-winning film director? Find out what inspired The Film Festival Doctor, Dr Rebekah Louisa Smith, to start up her own company, and why being considered a 'niche' is holding female filmmakers back.

When did your love affair with movies begin?
When I was 12 years old and saw *Pulp Fiction* for the first time. It was on a satellite television channel and I was glued to Tarantino's engaging dialogue, characters and his stylish and unique violence – no one can ever surpass his style.

Your PhD thesis was on Quentin Tarantino films. What draws you to his films in particular?
First and foremost, his characters – what they say, what they do and their way of living are awesome, plus they feel extremely real, funny and unpretentious.
I love the Madonna conversation in *Reservoir Dogs* and the 'Royale with Cheese' conversation in *Pulp Fiction.* I'm not a fan of fast food but every time I hear that conversation it makes me laugh!

What inspired you to start your company, The Film Festival Doctor?
I was co-producing a festival in Wales called the Abertoir Horror Festival when I realized how much I loved working within this

area. It was in fact the filmmakers who were attending the festival who inspired me to start my company, as they needed help.
The problem that needed solving (and that I could solve) was that there were no companies offering specific services to create a successful festival strategy and work with them as part of their team to get their films into festivals worldwide.

Why is entering awards important for filmmakers?
For a filmmaker who wins any type of legitimate award, this will raise their profile amongst their film industry peers and help them build a desirable image.
Also, if a short filmmaker wins an Oscar-qualifying award (at an Oscar-qualifying film festival) this means they can submit their film to be considered for an Oscar.
This is exactly what happened to the brilliant filmmakers behind the UK short film *The Silent Child,* who won the top prize at the Rhode Island Film Festival and then went on to win the Oscar.

You've helped your clients win over 800 awards. Do you have any advice to help creatives succeed in festivals and awards?
Yes – the golden rule is to always create a streamlined and focused festival strategy.
It's important to know your film and which type of festivals around the world would be interested in it. Taking a scattergun approach that is not in alignment with your goals and your film's strengths will not be successful.

What's your all-time favorite movie, and why?
To this day my favorite film is still (and will always be) *Pulp Fiction*! The characters, dialogue and quality of filmmaking never feels dated and it gets better every time I see it.

Your own business is predominantly female-led. What holds women back in the film industry, and what more can be done

to help them?

Yes indeed! I have an amazing female team supporting me, for which I'm truly grateful. I think the main thing holding women filmmakers back in the industry is being perceived as an overall 'niche'.

There are, for example, some great female director-focused film festivals and I'm a big fan of them. However, I'd like to see the general film festivals' Best Director categories for short films, feature films and documentary films to include both women and men. I'd like to phase out the Best Female Director category and let them compete with their male counterparts.

What's the biggest obstacle you personally have had to overcome?

Having my business being taken seriously by my peers – there was only a handful of companies around the world offering a similar service to me when I launched it during 2011.

A lot of people I met told me it wouldn't work as it was far too niche and no one would be able to afford it. Both those criticisms were limiting beliefs and I firmly believe that one can work around limiting beliefs and you can always turn this type of negativity around, so that's what I set out to do and I'm glad I have now overcome those obstacles.

You lecture and mentor at Middlesex University. What's the top piece of advice you offer aspiring filmmakers and writers?

I always tell them to dream big and that anything is possible. I'm a firm believer in goal setting and teach them that they need to plan their goals – I advise them to work backwards by identifying what their ultimate goal is (e.g. becoming an Oscar-winning director) and then breaking that big goal down into smaller goals. I also advise them to create daily goals so they can begin taking the small stepping stones towards the bigger goal.

Who inspires you?
Aside from my mother, I love Caprice – she's a phenomenal businesswoman who has demonstrated that she's not just a pretty model but one of the most hard-working women in the world. Her energy is infectious and genuine and, like me, she's always thinking of new ways to solve problems for her clientele.

Where would you like to be in five years' time?
Enjoying living and working hard in my favorite city, Los Angeles. I will also have established my brand further in the USA and supported an abundance of American-based filmmakers to achieve their goals and become successful in their careers.

www.talentedladiesclub.com

RESOURCES AND CONTACTS

Ed J.C. Smith, Champion Academy

Website: www.championacademy.co.uk

Email: ed@championacademy.co.uk

'Clients on Automation' Online Coaching Course: edjcsmithonlinemembershipsite.mykajabi.com

Facebook: www.facebook.com/edjcsmith

Ellen Watts

Website: www.be-unlimited-with-ellen-watts.com

Email: ewatts@ellerich.co.uk

Gerlanda Milioto

Website: www.linkedin.com/in/gerlandamilioto

Email: gerlanda.milioto@gmail.com

Marie Diamond

Website: mariediamond.com

Email: office@mariediamond.com

Marie Diamond's Quantum Colors Course:
mariediamond.com/diamond-quantum-colors-home-study-course

Nand Harjani

Website: www.creativelifesciences.com

Email: information@creativelifesciences.com

Butterfly House Publishing

Website: www.butterflyhousepublishing.com

REFERENCES

Books

Christopher Holland – *Film Festival Secrets: The Ultimate Handbook for Independent Filmmakers*. Stomp Tokyo.

Ed J.C. Smith – *Money Mindfulness Daily: What School Failed to Teach You.*

Ellen Watts – *Cosmic Ordering Made Easier. How to Get More of What You Want - More Often*. Wilson King Publishing, UK.

Jen Sincero – *You Are a Badass at Making Money: Master the Mindset of Wealth*. John Murray Learning, USA.

Jen Sincero – *You Are a Badass: How to Stop Doubting Your Greatness and Start Living an Awesome Life*. John Murray Learning, USA.

K. Souder and L. Rester – *The Soul Purpose Method: Discover Your Unique Calling, Reawaken to Your True Self, and Co-create the Inspired Life You Were Meant to Live*. Creos Company.

Louise L. Hay – *You Can Heal Your Life*. Hay House, UK.

Rhonda Byrne – *The Secret*. Simon & Schuster, UK.

Rob Moore – *I'm Worth More: Realize Your Value. Unleash Your Potential*. John Murray Learning, USA.

Websites

Bella Sorella – www.bellasorella.co.uk

Bluebella – www.bluebella.com

How to Find Your Soul Purpose, Amanda Linette Meder – www.amandalinettemeder.com

How to Create an Empowering Vision Board, Jack Canfield – www.jackcanfield.com/blog/how-to-create-an-empowering-vision-book

Natural Health – www.naturalhealthmagazine.co.uk

Silk Fred – www.silkfred.com

Soul & Spirit – www.soulandspiritmagazine.com

Spirit & Destiny – www.spiritanddestiny.co.uk

Made in the USA
Columbia, SC
24 October 2020